Building Enterprise
Information Architectures

Hewlett-Packard Professional Books

Blinn	Portable Shell Programming: An Extensive Collection of Bourne Shell Examples
Cook	Building Enterprise Information Architectures
Costa	Planning and Designing High Speed Networks Using 100VG-AnyLAN, Second Edition
Fristrup	USENET: Netnews for Everyone
Fristrup	The Essential Web Surfer Survival Guide
Grady	Practical Software Metrics for Project Management and Process Improvement
Grosvenor, Ichiro, O'Brien	Mainframe Downsizing to Upsize Your Business: IT-Preneuring
Gunn	A Guide to NetWare® for UNIX®
Helsel	Graphical Programming: A Tutorial for HP VEE
Kane	PA-RISC 2.0 Architecture
Knouse	Practical DCE Programming
Lewis	The Art & Science of Smalltalk
Malan, Letsinger, Coleman	Object-Oriented Development at Work: Fusion In the Real World
Madell, Parsons, Abegg	Developing and Localizing International Software
Malan	Object-Oriented Development at Work: Fusion in the Real World
McMinds/Whitty	Writing Your Own OSF/Motif Widgets
Phaal	LAN Traffic Management
Poniatowski	The HP-UX System Administrator's "How To" Book
Poniatowski	HP-UX 10.x System Administration "How To" Book
Thomas	Cable Television Proof-of-Performance: A Practical Guide to Cable TV Compliance Measurements Using a Spectrum Analyzer.
Witte	Electronic Test Instruments
Witte	Spectrum & Network Measurements

Building Enterprise Information Architectures

Reengineering Information Systems

Melissa A. Cook
Hewlett-Packard Company

For book and bookstore information

http://www.prenhall.com

Prentice Hall PTR
Upper Saddle River, NJ 07458

Library of Congress Cataloging-in-Publication Data

Cook, Melissa A.
    Building enterprise information architectures: reengineering
    information systems / Melissa A. Cook.
        p. cm. — (Hewlett-Packard professional books)
    Includes bibliographical references and index.
    ISBN 0-13-440256-1 (pbk.)
    1. Information technology—Management. 2. Business—Data processing. 3.
    Information storage and retrieval systems—Business.
    I. Title. II. Series.
    HD30.2.C656 1996
    658.4´038—dc20   95-42609
                                                                      CIP

Editorial/production supervision: *BooksCraft, Inc., Indianapolis, IN*
Cover design director: *Jerry Votta*
Cover design: *Carol Ceraldi*
Acquisitions editor: *Karen Gettman*
Manager Hewlett-Packard Press: *Patricia Pekary*
Manufacturing manager: *Alexis R. Heydt*

© 1996 by Prentice-Hall PTR
Prentice-Hall, Inc.
Upper Saddle River, New Jersey 07458

The publisher offers discounts on this book when ordered in bulk quantities.
For more information, contact:

> Corporate Sales Department
> Prentice Hall PTR
> One Lake Street
> Upper Saddle River, NJ 07458
> Phone: 800-382-3419   Fax: 201-236-7141
> E-mail: corpsales@prenhall.com.

All product names mentioned herein are the trademarks of their respective owners.

Printed in the United States of America

10 9 8

ISBN: 0-13-440256-1

PRENTICE-HALL INTERNATIONAL (UK) LIMITED, *LONDON*
PRENTICE-HALL OF AUSTRALIA PTY. LIMITED, *SYDNEY*
PRENTICE-HALL CANADA INC., *TORONTO*
PRENTICE-HALL HISPANOAMERICANA, S.A., *MEXICO*
PRENTICE-HALL OF INDIA PRIVATE LIMITED, *NEW DELHI*
PRENTICE-HALL OF JAPAN, INC., *TOKYO*
PEARSON EDUCATION ASIA PTE. LTD., *SINGAPORE*
EDITORA PRENTICE-HALL DO BRASIL, LTDA., *RIO DE JANEIRO*

Most problems have already been solved in this world, we just keep forgetting the solutions.

To Jesse and Savannah.

Table of Contents

Foreword

There are three reasons why I would consider Melissa Cook's *Building Enterprise Information Architectures* to be one of the substantive, "must read" books of the times.

First, Melissa has taken an arcane subject, "enterprise modeling," and made it so clear and intuitively obvious that it is embarrassing to realize how primitive our approaches have been for so many years. If that isn't embarrassing enough, she observes that the basic concepts have been around since Aristotle! Classification theory, which is at the heart of every kind of model, when applied correctly, produces enterprise designs that make a lot of sense and solve a lot of problems. I have read a lot of books and articles about enterprise engineering, re-engineering, and the like, but this is the first time I have read anything that tells how to do it so the resultant enterprise will actually work.

I really like Melissa's "home-style" dialog and down-to-earth analogies that cut through the fog of technological jargon and computer mythology to get to bare fact and plain truth. She states obvious realities, bursting the illusory bubbles of many popular fantasies, but it is all done with a wonderful sense of humor that makes the book not only readable but also entertaining.

The second reason this is a great book is because it can easily be read by someone who has no knowledge of information or systems or computers or technology. That is, it is a book for enterprise management. It makes simple a lot of complex technical subjects and dispels a lot of the mystery surrounding the systems domain. Personally, I usually say, "this is a physics problem, not mysticism—you need an architect, not a magician!" Melissa really reinforces this observation. Everything makes sense. It simply requires an understanding of some basic concepts and the determination and commitment to be faithful to them.

The fact that this book is a book for managers is incredibly significant. We are living in times of wrenching, underlying changes to all the
structures of the past—social, economic, political, environmental, and so
on. Alvin Toffler, in his seminal work, *Future Shock,* observes: "Knowledge is change—and accelerating knowledge-acquisition, fueling the
great engine of technology, means accelerating change." These times are
pivotal in the history of humanity. They are every bit as far reaching and
earth shattering as the industrial revolution. It is my opinion that as we
enter into this new age of knowledge and change, no longer do we have
the luxury of informality and complete spontaneity. Metaphorically, we
simply can't build hundred-story buildings starting with an ax and a for-
est of trees.

We must start with some standard components and an understanding of enterprise architecture. It is our only hope. Management must be
sufficiently conversant with architectural principles to make a substantive, knowledgeable contribution. Managers may never actually build the
architectural models, but they must know enough to recognize what the
models are expressing to them in order to make the trade-off decisions
that produce and change the enterprise for serving the purpose they
have in mind. I simply cannot see how any enterprise of any size at all
can be a serious player in the "Knowledge Age" without a management
knowledgeable about enterprise architecture. *Building Enterprise Information Architectures* is an easy entry into the realm of enterprise architecture and it provides an intellectual foundation for this vital
management expertise.

The third reason this is a great book is that it is a substantive contribution to the technical community as well. Although the book can be
easily read and understood by someone with little, if any, modeling experience or inclination, it is profound and revealing, even for the most
sophisticated I/S modeling professional. The book may be simple, but it is
not simplistic. It may be conceptual, but it is not abstract. It may be nontechnical, but it is not superficial. It is an in-depth, pragmatic look at
good modeling principles that, if applied correctly, could have an enor-
mously positive impact on our ability to produce results and resolve some
of the frustration that many enterprises have with their current inventory of information systems—the "legacy."

In fact, had we employed the concepts and principles outlined in
Building Enterprise Information Architectures for the last fifty years, we
likely would not have a "legacy" to contend with today.

Building Enterprise Information Architectures is a business book about information systems, not an information systems book about business. The principles Melissa expounds are timeless, and I expect that this book will be read by managers and I/S professionals for many years to come.

I think you will both have fun and learn a lot from Melissa Cook in *Building Enterprise Information Architectures.*

John A. Zachman
Glendale, California

Preface

There is nothing mysterious about information processing. Information processing has been at the heart of human existence since the dawn of civilization. It may surprise you that some of the first concepts examined and developed by early Greek scholars such as Plato are information processing fundamentals. While they certainly didn't discuss UNIX versus Windows NT, over two thousand years ago they developed concepts such as classification theory, which is the foundation of today's commercial information processing. Concepts developed later in civilization, such as the idea of standards, are also information processing fundamentals. Information processing is not a new field of expertise, and people who do not carry around the latest copy of *Computerworld* in their briefcases need not be intimidated by it.

Granted, these information processing fundamentals could have been utilized to provide a framework to allow component-oriented, interoperable commercial information systems forty years ago. But with all the excitement over the technological breakthroughs that computers continue to provide, it is probably excusable that we allowed some of those years to go by before we got back to basics.

You might also be able to excuse commercial software providers since competition would be a lot more fierce in a plug-and-play, commodity-based marketplace. Instead, we are all held hostage by the unique and proprietary approaches taken by all commercial software providers—the largest of which are hidden away in almost every Fortune 1000 company.

The first data processing departments were called that for a reason. The business views of your enterprise information architecture should be based on the data and processes necessary to run your business—it's as simple as that. It has nothing to do with technology. You do not have to be a computer scientist to define the business views of your enterprise information architecture. If you do not understand your data and processing needs, you have larger problems in your business than we will deal with in this book. It's time for members of the business management community to pick up the reins of the runaway technology stagecoach and get reacquainted with the data and processes that run their companies.

Why are current enterprise information systems architectures so complicated? Where did that spaghetti network of hundreds, in some companies thousands, of applications come from? For some reason, as we moved from manual information processing in the enterprise to automated information processing using more and more complex technology, the simple concepts behind information processing were lost. The word "information" now conjures up mental pictures of computing equipment. Technical jargon and the latest buzzwords have led business managers to believe that they can no longer understand their information processing needs. Confused by the new generation of computer whiz kids, they reluctantly relinquished control of their processes and information until it is now buried in millions of dollars of incomprehensible computing hardware and software. Slowly but surely the enterprise has become riddled with complexity and redundancy as many business managers feel helplessly overwhelmed by the computing quagmire.

The basic concepts behind information processing are still applicable. With simple discussions about the information and processing needs of the enterprise, an enterprise information architecture emerges to provide the structure to simplify, streamline, and regain control over business information and automated processes.

People who have been part of a previous enterprise information architecture project will be skeptical. Most enterprise information architecture design projects have failed. They rarely get completed or, if completed, rarely get implemented. Why is this?

Business leadership is an absolute requirement for developing and implementing an enterprise information architecture. However, most architecture projects have been delegated to the information technology community because the business community has been convinced that it can't possibly understand information processing anymore. The architecture then gets mired in technical details that business management can't comprehend, and projects lose their sponsorship and momentum and eventually are canceled.

The information technology community is obviously a critical partner in building an enterprise information architecture. But would you put one of your contractors in charge of the architectural drawing for your new office building? Of course not. You would hire an architect to design the architecture. You would also hire contractors and trust them to select the appropriate tools and materials based on their expertise and experience and encourage them to give the architect advice about potential architectural changes that would make it easier to build the building.

Business leadership for enterprise information architecture development is a must because only the business leaders understand the true information and processing needs of the enterprise. It is also a must because it will require executive-level understanding and commitment to manage the conflicts that inevitably occur when moving from an autonomous free-for-all to a controlled and coordinated approach.

This book describes the nontechnical view of enterprise information architectures. We have spent billions and billions of dollars throwing technology at redundant processes and information hoping for productivity improvement miracles but in the end creating confusion and chaos. This certainly does not mean that technology is unimportant in today's enterprise. In fact, businesses that figure out how to deploy new technology effectively and efficiently will have a significant advantage over competitors who don't. The framework that an enterprise information architecture provides reduces the complexity of information systems and enables the enterprise to effectively and efficiently deploy new technology.

Very few executives would allow key enterprise assets to be uncontrolled. For example, equipment, material, and real estate assets are tightly controlled in most companies. However, because software and high technology are still considered mysterious, most computing investments are treated by business managers as hopeful vials of snake oil. Since they can't understand it, information processing decisions are delegated to witch doctors in the information technology (IT) community who begin chanting technology buzzwords and shaking rattles made out of silicon. Although the cost of high technology probably makes it the largest asset in the enterprise, the normal asset management processes have been scared off.

High technology and the computing infrastructure must be positioned as an expensive enterprise asset under strict business control. Business control does not imply comprehensive business management understanding of all the details of the computing infrastructure any more than it implies detailed understanding of every piece of machinery in the enterprise. Business control over the computing assets is exercised through an enterprise information architecture.

Much like designing a home, executives play the role of homeowner and must work with an architect to provide an agreed upon architectural drawing for the information and processes in the enterprise. This high-level architectural drawing does not change with tactical decisions to deploy improved technology since it is simply built around a framework of business processes and the information that they need. At the lowest level of the architecture, much like deciding what type of lumber to use, the technologists define the tactics and are given free rein to apply the latest and greatest technology to the framework within financial constraints. Since most enterprises have existing information systems, the architectural drawing provides the future state and facilitates the best possible strategy to remodel with the least amount of inconvenience to the business.

Without a plan, anything will fail. Business management is guilty of not providing a plan for the information systems community to follow. This plan needs to be in the format of an information systems architecture. However, it has only been in the last few decades that an easy-to-understand methodology to design information architectures has emerged. The methodology was created primarily from work done by John Zachman, who first developed the concepts of information systems architectures, and information engineering pioneers such as Clive Finkelstein and James Martin. The Zachman framework provides for a set of architectural views from high-level business views to detailed, technical views. The business views provide the strategic plan with the lower levels fleshing out the tactical plan. This book will discuss only the business views of the architecture because of their importance in setting strategy.

Enterprise information architectures provide a framework for reducing information system complexity and enabling enterprise information sharing. There are also some significant technology benefits that flow out of an enterprise information architecture such as reducing data and software redundancy and facilitating the movement to new technology such as client/server or object-oriented systems.

This book is intended to be used as a reference for anyone interested in making more effective use of computers in commercial enterprise. Since it is critical to have both business and information systems personnel involved in the development of an architecture, easy to understand overviews of technical and business concepts are provided to allow both technical and business readers to understand each other's points of view.

Much of what is needed to build an enterprise information architecture has already been defined decades ago, in some cases, thousands of years ago. It is critical that this be synthesized and summarized so that business management can have a better understanding of how to manage technology deployment in the commercial enterprise. This book attempts to fill in that gap.

Claude Shannon of MIT, the creator of information theory in 1948,[1] said that a message has maximum information content when it is maximally "surprising." I hope that this book surprises you by demonstrating how simple commercial information processing really is.

1. Hans Moravec, *Mind Children, the Future of Robot and Human Intelligence*, 1988, p. 63.

Acknowledgments

First and foremost, to Dick Warmington for his continual encouragement, support, and sponsorship of this project.

To Judy Kincaid for her wealth of experience and personal support. It is a rare privilege to find both a business colleague and a great friend in the same person.

To the Hewlett-Packard Company for its support and encouragement of women in technical and management positions.

To John Zachman for his encouragement and his many, many years of experience in this area.

To Evergreen Software Tools, Inc., of 15444 NE 95th Street, Redmond, Washington, who provided EasyCASE® Professional™ v4.2 to create all of the data models in this book.

And lastly, to all my family and friends, who have patiently awaited the completion of this book.

Building Enterprise

Information Architectures

Historical Perspective

Information processing has been around since the dawn of human civilization. Thousands of years of thought and innovation have improved and influenced the information processing industry beginning as early as the fifth century B.C. Computers have entered the picture only in the last fifty years or so, really a tiny blip in the history of information processing. For over two thousand years, civilization has studied information and found better ways to process it in order to simplify daily living. There is such a heavy emphasis today on technology as the panacea for all information processing problems that we have lost our perspective, especially in the commercial world. It is technomyopia to assume that computers came before the idea of information processing. There have always been information and processes and always will be. Whether you use a $300,000 computer or a quill and scroll of papyrus is irrelevant in the grand scheme of information processing.

1.1 EARLY TOOLS FOR INFORMATION PROCESSING

This is not to say that the invention of new tools has not enabled us to make giant leaps in our ability to process information. The invention of the abacus around 500 B.C. and paper in 100 A.D. could certainly be considered as significant technical contributions to the information processing industry. More recent historical milestones in the information processing area include the invention of the steam-powered calculating machine shown in Figure 1–1 by Charles Babbage in 1834 and electro-mechanical calculators by Herman Hollerith of the United States in the

1

Figure 1–1
Machine constructed from drawings made by Charles Babbage (from *Charles Babbage and His Calculating Machines*, Dover Publications, 1961)

1890s, Leonardo Torres y Quevedo of Spain in 1919, and Konrad Zuse of Germany in 1934.

Herman Hollerith's invention is an interesting story. It took until 1887 to tally the results of the 1880 census, and it was estimated that in

1890 the tabulation would last until after 1900. Herman's company was awarded a contract to build an electromechanical tabulating machine to speed up the process. If you find stock in Herman's company in your grandmother's attic, keep it. Herman Hollerith's company grew into IBM.[1]

Certainly, we've come a long way since the days of the abacus and even Herman's incredible invention. The advent of early computers and eventually microprocessors, or computers on a chip, dramatically increased the potential for accuracy and speed. However, commercial information processing hasn't seemed to be able to take full advantage of all that potential. Although computers are certainly extremely fast, approaching a trillion operations per second, the number of operations necessary to keep the proliferation of information systems working in the enterprise is increasing at an even faster pace. Not only is this proliferation sucking up all that new hardware power and speed, it is decreasing the accuracy and speed of the business processes. Faster hardware will not fix our commercial information processing problems. Somewhere in the history of commercial computing lie the reasons why.

1.2 THE HISTORY OF COMPUTING

Most of what we think of today as the first generation of computers were birthed in hushed rooms full of mysterious blinking lights and people in white lab coats. The general public probably thought of them in the same way they think of the control room of a nuclear power plant today—definitely "hands off" for most of us. I doubt that anyone dreamed that computers would end up in children's classrooms. They were scientific inventions, tools for very smart engineers and scientists. As an aside, this gene pool is probably why the computer industry hasn't quite figured out the idea of "user-friendly." With (literally) rocket scientists as customers, who cared about user-friendly technology? Commands like prlp, cmds, and lstfl didn't seem all that unusual to that crowd. Unfortunately, rocket scientists are not the target audience for the majority of today's commercial computers, so what's with that autoexec.bat and slogon.ini stuff?

Like many machines that at first are considered to be experimental, computers saw much of their earliest usage by the military. Many of these military computer installations were top secret creations during World War II, leading to an even more mysterious aura around computing technology. This may be one of the reasons why there was originally

1. Hans Moravec, *Mind Children, the Future of Robot and Human Intelligence,* pp. 66-7.

little discussion about processes and data. No one outside of a small and elite group was supposed to know what these computers were doing. These original computer customers are still some of the world's largest computer customers today. They magnetically erase their disc drives, swear everyone to secrecy, and still break out in a sweat when they let the service person in the door.

Historically speaking, the first generation of computers are commonly considered to be those that were developed around the vacuum tube toward the end of World War II when governments invested billions on computing hardware and software used primarily for code breaking and weapon design. This kind of activity really underwrote the emergence of today's hardware and software industry. Some sophisticated software originally built for the military is still around, recycled for commercial applications. As an example, parts of the automobile industry still simulate auto crashes on a software program originally designed to answer an important question of the day: What would happen to a bomb casing if the plane carrying it crashed?[2] As an aside, I wonder what the answer to that question is since one would think the laws of physics apply whether you drop a bomb with or without the plane attached.

The 1960s ushered in the second generation of computers, which used transistors. This generation was the catalyst for the frenzy that we are so familiar with in successive generations, creating computers that were smaller, cheaper, and faster, faster, faster. The third generation quickly emerged in the late 1960s with hybrid integrated circuitry where unpackaged transistors and other components were bonded onto ceramic chips. This generation made a lot of significant breakthroughs, and eventually components were etched directly into silicon. A fourth generation evolved into the microprocessor generation where a complete computer was put on a single chip. The computer industry eventually gave up on generation numbering since there are so many miraculous advances every year[3]. It doesn't make sense to call it a generation when the gap is only a few months long.

1.2.1 The Computer and Human Intelligence

Certainly high technology has made it possible to process incredible amounts of information. Many people think that the computer is getting

2. Russell Mitchell, "Fantastic Journeys in Virtual Labs," *Business Week*, September 19, 1994: 80.

3. Moravek, p. 67.

close to the ability to mimic human intelligence itself. Hans Moravec, in his 1988 book *Mind Children, the Future of Robot and Human Intelligence*, makes an indirect conclusion as to the size of computer that would be needed to mirror the brain's complexity with artificial intelligence. A direct conclusion is obviously not possible in his opinion, since we still have a rather naive understanding about both the brain and the future vision of computing. However, Moravec takes a stab at it by comparing the human retina to computer vision programs. He then extrapolates that comparison to the whole brain which has approximately a 1:10,000 ratio of complexity between retina and brain. His calculations indicate that you would have to have a computer that could process ten trillion operations per second and have ten trillion words of memory. He is very clear that this is probably a rash conclusion. But basing additional calculations on historical progress in computing, he predicts that we could look forward to the potential of a $10 million supercomputer mimicking human intelligence before 2010 and a $1,000 personal computer doing so by 2030. Maybe these super brains really *can* solve all our information processing problems in the enterprise. Maybe it's a higher priority to start coordinating our vacation plans so we don't all move to Tahiti on the same day.

As a testament to the miraculous speed of technology breakthroughs, the September 19, 1994, *Business Week* article entitled "Fantastic Journeys in Virtual Labs" indicates that the type of computer Moravec expected to exist in 2010 looks like it will be here before the year 2000. "By 1996, the curtain will rise on the next act—a new type of supercomputer dubbed 'teraops.' At peak speed, these machines will chew through at least a trillion operations per second or teraops—10 to 50 times as many as today's best number crunchers. Such fantastic speeds are essential for tackling so-called Grand Challenge problems. These are the knottiest puzzles facing science, such as developing fusion-energy reactors and understanding the global climate."

Most of us who are business managers aren't too worried about developing fusion-energy reactors and understanding the impact of global warming. We have more simple goals. We'd just like to be able to manufacture the product, take the order, ship the goods, and have the customer's purchase order match the invoice without requiring armies of administrators and Herculean effort.

Another author, Christopher Evans, also compares the computer to living things, but he doesn't think that we're approaching human intelligence very quickly. In his opinion, all intelligence, living or not, can be measured by six factors: data capture ability, data storage capability, processing speed, software flexibility, software efficiency, and software range. In the 1980s, he put computers somewhere near the tapeworm on the intelligence range and suggested that, in the 1990s, they would potentially surpass the hedgehog.[4] Maybe an ambitious goal would be to have computers surpass Homer Simpson sometime in the next few centuries.

Author Hubert Dreyfus isn't quite so convinced that computers can be compared to living intelligence at all.

In the period between the invention of the telephone relay and its apotheosis in the digital computer, the brain, always understood in terms of the latest technological inventions, was understood as a large telephone switchboard or, more recently, as an electronic computer. This model of the brain was correlated with work in neurophysiology which found that neurons fired a somewhat all or nothing burst of electricity. This burst, or spike, was taken to be the unit of information in the brain corresponding to the bit of information in a computer. This model is still uncritically accepted by practically everyone NOT directly involved with work in neurophysiology, and underlies the naive assumption that man is a walking example of a successful digital computer program.[5]

Dreyfus additionally sums up some later work in 1966 by Walter Rosenblight of MIT, one of the pioneers in the use of computers in neuropsychology: "Thus the view that the brain, as a general purpose symbol-manipulating device, operates like a digital computer, is an empirical hypothesis which has had its day."

We need to stop waiting for technology to magically solve the human side of our commercial information processing problems. Without an information processing framework or architecture within which to apply them, faster processors are probably going to make things worse in the enterprise, not better.

1.3 SCIENTIFIC VERSUS COMMERCIAL COMPUTING

Most of our commercial information processing problems have to do with transacting business between humans by collecting information and moving it through a business process. Scientific organizations worry about solving complex mathematical problems such as simulating com-

4. *The Micro Millennium*, 1979, p. 165.
5. *What Computers Still Can't Do: A Critique of Artificial Reason*, 1992, p. 159.

plex situations like the global climate. In scientific organizations, before the advent of computers, many of these large mathematical algorithms were incalculable by humans. For example, the computer could suddenly calculate pi to thousands of decimals in a fraction of a second, a useful fact to someone hidden away in the bowels of the Pentagon, no doubt. Computers were held in very high esteem in scientific organizations because of their demonstrated ability to calculate better and faster than humans.

Commercial computing had a much more humble beginning and has not gained quite as positive a reputation. So far, it is questionable to some executives whether the computer is an improvement from a cost and efficiency standpoint over all those file clerks of yesteryear. What happened to computers in commercial industry?

1.3.1 A Historical Lack of Line Management Involvement in Commercial Computing

As computers established themselves as more than experimental scientific devices, the commercial world began to take a look at the possibilities, although they were still quite skeptical as to the value of this newfangled device. The commercial world does not have its roots in the scientific quest for knowledge, and experiments do not have quite the same connotation in corporate culture. This is probably what led to the computer being quickly relegated to the administrative side of the house—sort of an industrywide "let Mikey try it." Where scientific organizations applied computers directly to the most pressing, unsolved problems, commercial organizations sidelined the computer into automating already solved, albeit manual, business problems such as administrative processes.

The first commercial application of computers was to automate accounts payable, accounts receivable, inventory, and general ledger for General Electric Company in 1954.[6] There were about 6,000 computers of this type by the end of the 1950s[7]. Commercial computing was primarily positioned to replace things that humans were already capable of doing, unlike military or scientific computing. The main emphasis in early commercial applications was on administrative tasks and was rarely something in the mainstream of the business. Right out of the starting block, commercial computers were not positioned to provide

6. Paul Tom, *Computer Information Systems, a Managerial Approach*, 1989, p. 6.
7. Moravek, p. 67.

business breakthroughs equivalent to those found by applying computers to scientific problems.

Commercial computers became key administrative assets but not key business assets since they were only indirect profit contributors. This was the beginning of today's serious problem in commercial computing— *a lack of direct line management involvement and understanding.* Most early computing decisions were made by administrators. Therefore, much of the current legacy computing infrastructure in most enterprises is administrative in nature, and line managers are not that involved. You can see this by looking at who uses the majority of today's commercial computers. I bet every administrator has a personal computer (PC) or a terminal, but does every line manager? If the line managers do have PCs or terminals, are they used as daily gateways into critical business information or do they use them primarily for stand-alone PC applications and nasty E-mail messages?

If you actually attempt to inventory your computing equipment, you will probably be unpleasantly surprised. Information technology and administrative departments probably have most of the computing equipment. In many companies, there is little left to give to line functions other than maybe hand-me-downs. Something is really backwards about this situation.

Certainly, administration is a key organization in the enterprise because it processes information on behalf of the line business. However, it is one step removed from the true business problems. The main business objective of most companies is not to administrate. A computing infrastructure built around the needs of administration is like talking through an interpreter. Key priorities can get lost. Even the most user-focused information technology teams in industry are still one step removed from the true business objectives since the majority of their users are administrative.

The failure of commercial information technology to achieve clear return on investment (ROI) is due to a simple problem—a lack of direct line management involvement and understanding to ensure that computers are managed and applied to high-priority business problems. If line management does not take direct control of the computing architecture, this problem will persist in the enterprise. Business managers are going to have to pick up the reins of this runaway stagecoach. It's not acceptable for business managers to continue to just sit there and complain about the bumpy ride.

1.3.2 The Toy Mentality

In addition to the lack of line management involvement and understanding in commercial computing, we seem to have taken an interesting detour when computers entered the commercial scene. For some reason, as complex high technology played an increased role in information processing, the emphasis and interest shifted from information processing improvement toward the technology itself. We are like children who know we are supposed to be on the way to school but we can't seem to get out of the candy store. Even the enterprise value system changed. We have an almost herolike worship of high-technology experts in our enterprise, and business people who are the real information processing experts have been waved off with impatience by the new techno-elite.

It may be because of what can be called the "toy mentality." Some of this technology stuff is fun. Even business people are getting caught up in it. Personal computers can be used for business transactions one minute and a game of Doom the next. Some people call this the Wintendo effect. If a person doesn't care for games, a computer can also satisfy the needs of closet technophiles who spend hours pouring through manuals, quietly gloating when they find a new feature that no one else around them knows about. Perhaps because there were hundreds of years between significant information processing inventions in ancient times, our enterprise ancestors were able to tire of the latest version of MS-Abacus and focus back on processing King Tut's order for more golden statues. "Hey you, stop playing with that abacus and tell UPS to get those chariots over here on the double." Perhaps today's wildfire pace of technology inventions keeps us, unlike our ancestors, from ever getting back to work. We are so fascinated over the latest bits and bytes and mips and chips that we start forgetting about those statues piling up by the door.

We even like to wow the boss with impressive prototypes of the latest computer technology even though we never quite get around to turning the demo into a working system. Making most of those impressive prototypes work would require us to have improved information and processes that don't yet exist in our enterprise. We're just like audiophiles who spend so much time buying and installing hi fi equipment that they don't have time to listen to any music except the demo CD of the *Grand Canyon Suite.*

We're perfectly willing to brag about these technotoys to our industry neighbors. We coyly mention the latest technology that we just installed but politely avoid discussions about how much better our process or information is now. The latest technology buzzword seems to stimulate more interest than the thought of having to actually address the business complexity provided from the last round of technology we threw into the quagmire. Discussions about multimedia, object oriented, client/server, and the latest graphical user interface (GUI) technology serve as conversation fillers at a giant industry cocktail party where no one wants to talk about boring topics like information and process, the stuff this technology is supposed to improve in a commercial enterprise.

1.4 BACK TO BASICS

Industry wide discussions will be necessary over time to better understand commercial information processing. Perhaps the reason we haven't already done this is the competitive nature of a free-market economy. Competition fuels secrecy which may have driven us to avoid public discussion about our commercial information and processes, the obvious guts to commercial information processing. Ari Onassis was once quoted as saying, "The secret of business is to know something that nobody else knows." Perhaps that attitude encourages us to outwardly focus only on technology and not on what it is doing in our enterprise. However, the latest and greatest technology is worthless in business unless it lets you process an order or track finished goods inventory better, faster, or cheaper.

Since the concept of information processing is over two thousand years old, it is likely that information processing tools will continue to evolve in ways we probably can't predict. Don't forget, the human brain and human hand are still the largest installed base of information processing tools in the world. There are still significant, potentially breathtaking breakthroughs in technology yet to come. Therefore, in the world of information processing, if you base the foundation of your information architecture on current technology, you are taking a very myopic viewpoint. Technology is a tactical tool for information processing—no more, no less. It is much more important that we clearly understand our information and processing needs so that we have a framework to quickly apply whatever the future holds for us.

The astute business manager will set an extremely high priority on defining the information and processes necessary to effectively run his or her organization. This is what becomes the business views of the enterprise information architecture. The business views provide the framework that controls the deployment of technology in the enterprise. It is the "what" of the architecture, not the "how." Maybe at some point, you'll just put your brain up to the side of a computer and that will be it. But your brain better be able to tell the computer what to do. By separating the business view of information processing from the technology view, we actually end up enabling faster technology deployment. Most current technology projects get bogged down because of the lack of understanding about process and information needs, not because the technology doesn't work.

1.5 MISSED OPPORTUNITIES

We really should be ashamed of ourselves. In the last twenty years, there have been many significant opportunities for commercial computing to get back on the right track. We actually started out in pretty good shape. While relegating commercial computing to administration took it outside the mainstream of the business, there were some positive outcomes of this reporting structure. The nature of administrative organizations facilitated tight control over all assets including the computer. In fact, in many cases, the data processing manager was the company controller. Although the idea of an information architecture had not really been developed at this stage, the computer was managed as an asset, and companies usually examined automation decisions more carefully to ensure that there was a return on investment.

However, in these early stages, enterprise-wide information architectures were very simplistic. Since computing was new, risky, and expensive and limited to the automation of a few administrative departments, very little data and software was redundant in the enterprise. Therefore, the importance of tightly managing the computing environment with an architectural framework was not yet obvious. In many cases, a single computer and a few applications comprised the entire information architecture.

As the number of applications grew, the centrally managed data processing department could easily identify multiple needs for the same data. Rather than creating redundant data, the concept of master files, such as the customer or product master, emerged and they were shared between batch applications by physically moving card decks or magnetic tapes from one application to another via sneaker-net (see Figure 1–2). This kept data and software redundancy to a minimum. With a small and centrally controlled data processing department, it was pretty easy to carefully manage the master files and key applications.

Figure 1–2
Sharing master files via sneakernet

As computing became more practical and cost efficient for commercial usage, many new applications were found in the enterprise. Two complications emerged in the enterprise. First, data processing departments rapidly grew in size because of the increasing numbers of software development projects. Second, processing needs soon exceeded the capacity of a single computer. Now, reliance on the single manager for consistency in the information architecture would no longer work. The increased number of people and computers in the data center led to more difficult coordination between project teams. Projects that would have originally shared data or logic because of a common manager or computer became decoupled, leading to creeping data and software redundancy.

Without an information architecture and its standards to provide guidance to all the disparate project teams, programmers were left to their own devices to solve their own particular problems. It became too difficult to try to coordinate projects with anyone else's. The pressing business problems still needed to be solved to satisfy the boss. Very quickly, the computing infrastructure started to get out of control. We would never accept this type of situation when building a complex high-rise or planned community. The size of the project would not be an acceptable excuse for all the contractors to do whatever they thought best. Can you imagine all the contractors just sort of guessing where they should lay concrete and build walls? In the area of information systems, what was missing was the concept of an architecture. It's really quite simple—an architecture provides the basis for business control over the contractors.

1.5.1 The Impact of Distributed Computing on Redundancy

With the increasing need for more processing throughput and faster application development, batch-oriented mainframes became enterprise bottlenecks. To meet these demands, the computer industry responded with the development of on-line transaction processing (OLTP) and distributed computing. These significant technological accomplishments allowed and encouraged a much more decentralized development approach resulting in faster application turnaround time to the users. They also increased throughput by moving the computing power closer to the business transaction, eventually all the way to the PC, a rather recent invention in the history of information processing.

Distributed computing and OLTP allowed more flexibility in reacting to urgent business problems. However, these combined technological advances created an uncontrolled explosion of redundant data and software in the enterprise. Predictably this led to chaos in the very departments technology was intended to streamline through automation. Into this chaotic environment, we wistfully continue to throw more capable and sophisticated technology like throwing money over our shoulders into a wishing well. This not only doesn't improve the situation but is like trying to herd a bunch of feral cats with F14s.

It's important to give some kudos to the computer industry at this point. Like many new ideas, the term "distributed computing" became a buzzword, and its true meaning was not always well understood. Distributed computing was truly a breakthrough idea. The computer industry always intended some critically important but mostly misunderstood differences between the notions of decentralized and distributed computing.

1.5.2 Decentralized versus Distributed Computing

Decentralized implies complete autonomy and independence. In 1982, John Nack from Caterpillar Tractor Company wrote:

> Let us first examine decentralization because it is the most straightforward and, in its purest sense, is not in my opinion a logical long-term alternative for most systems or most companies....A decentralized operation usually implies a number of relatively small data centers independently providing relatively small portions of the organization's overall processing needs....If it is determined that there

is a need to coordinate or communicate among these independent entities, it will quickly be determined that there is also a need for some form of central control or management....Most importantly, it begins to lead toward the establishment of a central authority, a concept more applicable to centralized or distributed processing.[8]

The central authority he is talking about is provided by an enterprise information architecture.

Obviously, the opposite of decentralized is centralized. A completely centralized approach can provide the same central authority that Nack suggested, but it has some large disadvantages which is why most companies are moving away from that model. Typically, in any reasonably large company, a centralized computing approach gets bogged down by its sheer size. Application turnaround time in a centralized data processing department is usually unacceptable, especially in highly competitive industries that demand a high rate of process change. This is not a reflection of the personnel in the centralized computing environment. In fact, most of them continue to be some of the most well-rounded experts in the company, although they may have lost their reputation in the demise of centralized computing. The best programmer in the world would find it hard to satisfy thousands of users with a single application.

Centralized development efforts of the past usually resulted in huge, complex, worldwide, mega-applications that attempted to satisfy everyone but had to settle for the average user who really didn't exist. Centralization was blamed for user dissatisfaction. But how much more satisfied are the business users now that we've decentralized computing?

The centralized organization, however, is not entirely without blame. The concept of a central authority that could have been provided by an enterprise architecture was not utilized even in central organizations. In many cases, application integration wasn't any better in a centralized environment than it is today in a decentralized environment. So when the users grabbed their computers and ran, there really wasn't any clear benefit of a central authority to prevent them from heading for the hills.

Although many people do not understand this, the concept of distributed processing is not that far away from the concept of centralization. Distribution implies division of a previous whole. The concept of

8. "Newton's Laws of Data Processing," *The Economics of Information Processing*, p. 20.

distributed computing is similar to Peter Drucker's management concept of federal decentralization.

> Any federal organization requires both strong parts and a strong center. The term "decentralization" is actually misleading—though far too common by now to be discarded. Federal decentralization requires strong guidance from the center through the setting of clear, meaningful and high objectives for the whole. The objectives must demand both a high degree of business performance and a high standard of conduct throughout the enterprise.[9]

Drucker's definition of federal decentralization is much like the concept of true distributed computing. While distributed computing is clearly not a physically centralized approach, it is a logically centralized approach. It implies a logical whole. It does not imply complete autonomy, and it demands the same central coordination intended by a centralized approach without the disadvantages of size. It is truly a breakthrough balance with the flexibility of decentralized computing and the coordination advantages of centralization, equivalent to Drucker's high business performance and high standard of conduct. For very good reason, distributed computing is here to stay. Even though computer users haven't experienced business productivity gains with the demise of centralized computing, don't expect them to come out of the hills and sheepishly return their computers to the water-cooled, raised-floor, air-conditioned computer center, although some people may secretly harbor those thoughts. They've got their computer and they'll never give it back. Therefore, we have to figure out how to coordinate a distributed approach to computing. This is the purpose of an enterprise information architecture.

Most companies would tell you that they use a distributed computing approach. However, the term "distributed computing" is erroneously used in most enterprises. It is normally used as an excuse for a decentralized free-for-all. Decentralized computing is really appropriate only for stand-alone and autonomous projects or departments. Perhaps some of your R&D organizations fit this bill. Unfortunately, most departments don't have the luxury of operating in a vacuum, apart from the rest of the enterprise. But most users have become so dissatisfied with the slow pace of the centralized computing organization that they have already

9. *The Practice of Management*, 1956, p.214.

thrown the baby of central coordination out with the bathwater of centralized computing bureaucracy.

The need to integrate information and processes didn't go away as users grabbed their piece of the computing pie. The need for coordinated enterprise information about customers and products didn't go away. Previous process and information gaps that already existed in the centralized environment became gaping holes in a distributed environment, requiring manual procedures, rework, redundancy, and spaghetti system linkages as fingers in the enterprise dike.

With the demise of centralized control fueled by decentralized computing masquerading as distributed computing, an information architecture could have continued to be the stabilizing and integrating factor for the enterprise. An enterprise information architecture provides the central authority and control necessary to effectively migrate from a controlled, centralized approach to a controlled but truly distributed approach to computing. Without it, distributed computing has little ability to achieve return on investment.

1.5.3 Database Management Systems

The problems being faced by most enterprises toying with distributed computing were not being ignored by the computer industry. Several very significant technical breakthroughs were made to provide the central authority and control needed to facilitate a smooth migration to a distributed approach to computing.

The advent of database management systems (DBMS) in the 1970s was intended to provide more central control over information and reduce data redundancy by allowing the sharing of a central database between applications that could be developed in a distributed fashion. Fundamentally, the idea of a DBMS retained a central information authority necessary to support effective distributed computing (see Figure 1–3). The applications could be distributed while the database would become the central authority. The key benefit provided by the DBMS approach was the ability to separate software (process) from data, eliminating the need for each application to have its own proprietary but redundant data.

However, a shared database would require more than one department or application development team to work together. Previously, most files were structured around the transaction or department that was processing it. Rather than data needs being defined by a single department and its transactions, DBMSs required a more enterprise-

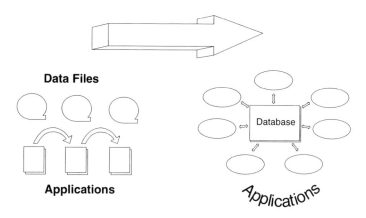

Figure 1–3
Intended implementation of DBMS technology

wide view of the data since multiple departments would be utilizing it. The first emergence of the idea of form over function or, as you will see later, Plato's concept of knowledge over opinion was subtly hidden in the idea of a DBMS.

As you undoubtedly know, team efforts are much more difficult than doing something yourself, and people naturally resisted the concept of a common database between projects. By the time DBMSs made their way into most enterprises, decentralized computing had led to the loss of control, and the key benefit of DBMSs was lost in the confusion. Most implementations of a DBMS today are just replacements of a single department's previous flat or indexed files—the proverbial paving of cow paths. Very few files belonging to separate applications or departments were merged into a shared database. Where there were three applications, there became three databases. This did not separate the application from the data in the sense intended by DBMS technology (see Figure 1–4).

In the book *The Economics of Information Processing*, published in 1982, Brandt Allan from the University of Virginia discusses the separation of data from process and the inability of most companies to take full advantage of DBMS without this separation. He states:

> Finally, one needs a separate data strategy. For if corporate information is not conceived of and planned independently of applications or technology, the organization will find it extremely difficult to achieve the full advantage of data base technology. Many users of this technology have been disappointed because it did not automatically result in the creation of company-wide or "global" files. Instead, they found

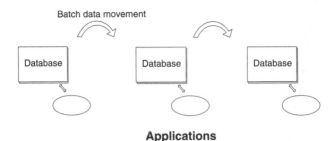

Applications

Figure 1–4
Typical implementation of DBMS technology does not separate application from data

themselves wedded to their traditional functional or localized data collections even after several years of experience with data base systems. (p. 10)

1.5.4 Data Dictionaries

Since most companies could not run on a single physical, enterprise-wide database even if they could pull off the political side, more progress was made in the 1980s when data dictionaries were developed to provide central control over data definitions while allowing decentralized database deployment. Where databases provided for shared data between multiple applications by providing a single database, data dictionaries added the ability to integrate multiple databases. The concept of a data dictionary provided an enterprise or holistic view of data since it would encompass all databases in the enterprise. The data dictionary would ensure that there were common definitions so data could be consolidated or synchronized between different physical databases. You could have a customer database as part of the marketing system and a customer database as part of the order processing system, but you would have the ability to coordinate the same customer record between the two or more databases. More forward-thinking implementations of data dictionaries would allow for common data definitions between vendor databases and customer databases since the same companies could appear in both. Perhaps it's not important to your company to be able to have an integrated view of all the relationships you have with a business partner, but certainly an enterprise view of a customer is important to most customer-oriented enterprises. Data dictionary technology continues to improve, but very few organizations have adopted and implemented enterprise data dictionaries because implementation requires some sort of central authority. Once again, a significant information processing advance has been pretty much ignored.

1.5.5 Information System Architectures

In September 1987, another breakthrough occurred when John Zachman published an important paper identifying what he called "A Framework for Information Systems Architecture," sometimes called the "Zachman framework."[10] This framework has become a de facto standard for enterprise information architecture design. Until this time, an easy-to-understand methodology for developing an enterprise information architecture didn't exist. Many scholars, pioneers, and consulting firms have emerged more recently to provide enhanced techniques and tools developed around this classic concept. Incredibly, most enterprises have very little knowledge about the Zachman framework, and it has been yet another sadly ignored breakthrough.

Zachman's breakthrough framework intended to provide a methodology to control decentralized chaos which was already here when his paper was written in 1987.

> In either case, since the technology permits "distributing" large amounts of computing facilities in small packages to remote locations, some kind of structure (or architecture) is imperative because decentralization without structure is chaos. Therefore, to keep the business from *dis*integrating, the concept of information systems architecture is becoming less an option and more a necessity for establishing some order and control in the investment of information system resources. (p. 276)

The Zachman framework and related approaches such as information engineering pioneered by Clive Finkelstein identify the need for a separate data, process, and technology architecture within the concept of an enterprise information architecture. Note that these approaches build upon the concept of separating process from data, earlier implemented through the idea of a DBMS.

In today's environment, each department or system usually has a vertically integrated approach to data, process, and technology. For example, department A has an application with its own database and runs on its own computer. Department B has another application with its own database and runs on its own computer. The same is true for depart-

---

10. *IBM Systems Journal* 26, no. 3, 1987.

ment C. The Zachman framework takes a 180-degree turn and moves from this vertical, departmental approach to a completely opposite horizontal approach, as shown in Figure 1–5. (We will refer to this illustration frequently throughout this book.) Data, process, and technology are looked at across the enterprise, each with its own characteristics. With the architected approach, you will find that the process architecture is built around activities (function), the data architecture is built around facts (form), and the technology architecture is built around physical constraints such as geography or hardware performance. For example, an architected approach may determine that departments A, B, and C have differing processes and therefore should have their own applications. However, department A's processes need data similar to department B's processes and therefore should share an integrated database. Departments A, B, and C are all in the same building, so they could all share a computer. The process, data, and technology architectural decisions are independent of each other.

All of these architectures are simultaneously developed by moving through sequential levels of detail or views. In addition, iterations can be expected as discoveries are made in lower levels of the architecture. This architectural iteration can be compared to designing a home. First, an architectural drawing is completed, but you may later discover that the plumbing schematic generated by the planned architecture of a

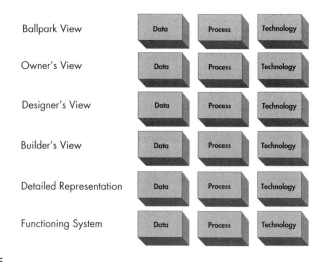

Figure 1–5
The basic Zachman framework approach to data, process, and technology

home would be too costly. When you simplify the plumbing schematic, it impacts the higher-level architectural view of the home, but now you have a better architecture and a better plumbing schematic.

It is a sad situation that the breakthroughs of distributed computing, DBMS, data dictionaries, and the Zachman framework have been pretty much ignored in commercial computing. The chaos in commercial computing could be solved by applying these concepts. And most of these concepts are built on time-tested information processing concepts from antiquity. What we need to provide an efficient, effective computing infrastructure already exists. There are no more excuses.

1.6 COMMERCIAL COMPUTING RETURN ON INVESTMENT?

After billions of dollars of investment, there is very little significant proof of return on investment in many commercial applications. The world's *first* computer customer, the U.S. government, is now the world's *largest* computer customer. It spends about $25 billion every year, about five percent of discretionary federal spending.[11] Remember Herman Hollerith's electromechanical tabulator for the U.S. Census Bureau? The first commercial computer system using vacuum tube technology was the Univac I, and its customer was the same U.S. Census Bureau.[12] (These days, we'd call that an installed base upgrade.) The U.S. Census Bureau has continued to upgrade like most enterprises. They spent $2.6 billion on the last census.[13] Interestingly enough, all that computing equipment that was predicted to create a paperless society hasn't slowed down the manufacture of file cabinets. The United States alone is still producing over 18 million brand new file cabinets a year, about five for every newborn baby.[14] Clearly, we have not yet harvested the enormous potential of computers in commercial information processing.

1.7 TAKE THE BUS TO THE FIFTH STATION

A colleague once described a wonderful analogy for tackling difficult tasks. It comes from the Pacific Rim and describes how to quickly get to

11. Cassandra Burrell, "Study: Feds Waste Billions on Computers," *Seattle Times*, October 12, 1994: A7.

12. Moravek, p. 67.

13. Mitch Betts, "Census 2000 Gears Up with Systems Overhaul," *Computerworld*, October 3, 1994: 4.

14. Arno Penzias, *Ideas and Information, Managing in a High-Tech World*, 1989.

the top of a tall mountain. It's pretty simple. Take the bus. The analogy really goes something like this: To climb the mountain, take the bus to the fifth and last station on the mountain's flanks before starting the final ascent to the peak (Figure 1–6).

Figure 1–6
Take the bus to the fifth station

Take the shortcut when building your enterprise information architecture. Take the bus to the fifth station. There is a lot of history, research, experience, and examples available to the enterprise information architect since the need to process information has existed since the apes stood up or Eve was created, whichever viewpoint you prefer. Isaac Newton once said, "If I have seen further, it is by standing upon the shoulders of Giants."

We also have a lot of giants to take advantage of when building an enterprise information architecture. Industry has an incredible propensity toward buzzwords that are really just slight changes to something that has been done before. Most of our questions have been answered; we just keep forgetting the answers. Perhaps giving new names for old techniques gives hope to the beleaguered business community, exhausted from trying the previous fad. I'm reminded of a quote by Tex Bender: "After weeks of beans and taters, even a change to taters and beans is good."[15]

15. *Don't Squat with Yer Spurs On! A Cowboy's Guide to Life*, 1992.

On the way to the fifth station, we will use concepts and experts from such unlikely sources as the dictionary, predicate logic, plant taxonomy, and Plato, in addition to more current concepts, such as the Zachman framework and database design. Again, information is a basic human concept and, since the dawn of civilization, many breakthroughs have been made. Perhaps because of the youth of most computing experts and excitement over the latest technology discovery, much of useful history that can be applied to information processing problems has been ignored. This book will try to take you to the fifth station. All aboard?

Gaining Support for an Enterprise Information Architecture

The single most difficult task in developing an enterprise information architecture is gaining support from the enterprise itself. That sounds a little strange, but going from a decentralized free-for-all to a coordinated approach to information systems development is a large paradigm shift. I mentioned earlier that there is no sense in even starting an architecture project if the architecture is not positioned as a business initiative. This is because only business management has any hope of getting and keeping support for a coordinated approach to systems development provided by an architecture. It will require executive-level commitment and tenacity. The information technology organization should not have to go tin cupping to its user community for support for an enterprise information architecture. If the business community cannot see the clear value of an enterprise information architecture, then the business is not yet ready for it. However, there are many things that can be done to educate business management to the point where they can see the value.

2.1 NATURAL RESISTANCE IN THE ENTERPRISE

Realistically, you will need to address ongoing resistance as part of life in an architected environment until the architecture becomes as well established as underground utilities. However, educating people on the benefits of an architecture and the standards it provides along with positioning it as a business initiative will scare off most naysayers save those that criticize anything that wasn't their idea to start with. Hopefully you've learned to ignore that group a long time ago or you have bigger problems than an architecture will fix.

An architecture does not at first seem to be in the best interest of internal information systems departments with their own proprietary approach to systems development, and there may be extreme resistance from these organizations, especially decentralized teams who have had complete freedom in the past. Where there has been strong sponsorship from a user community in the development of departmental systems, the users will join the fray in resisting the central coordination necessary for an architecture. This is why an enterprise information architecture requires so much business management leadership, involvement, and commitment. This is not a project for wimps.

2.2 ENTERPRISE ARCHITECTURES PRIMARILY PROVIDE STANDARDS

You can think of an enterprise information architecture as providing primarily a set of enterprise information processing standards. We are not talking about technology standards like networking protocols, although those are certainly important to the lower levels of the architecture. Standards that are provided by the business views of the enterprise information architecture ensure that processes and information can be interconnected across departments, just like coupling garden hoses together.

Standards are not a new idea. Let's take the bus.

2.3 🚐 A HISTORICAL PERSPECTIVE ON STANDARDS

We are surrounded by standards. Standard Time, standard clothing sizes, standard light bulb wattage, standard battery sizes, even standard movie seat specifications. Thank goodness, today you can consistently expect to find the brake pedal to the left of the gas pedal. There are now over 94,000 standards in the United States alone.

Most of the standards we know of today emerged as part of the industrial age. Previously, craftsmen took pride in doing everything themselves, sort of like a decentralized information systems community. The industrial age led to the idea of the division of labor to allow for mass production. This division of labor led to specialization—you put that widget in and I'll put the next one in. But, and that's a big but, everything was still expected to work together at the end of the assembly line. Standards were put in place to allow mass production when craftsmen just couldn't keep up with demand, just the sort of situation we have in most current information systems organizations.

The departmentalization of an enterprise is basically the same idea as the division of labor on an assembly line. You do the marketing, you do the manufacturing, and I'll do the distribution. However, standards have never been put in place to increase cooperation, information exchange, and productivity across departments. This leads to chaos at the end of the information assembly line.

We would never put up with this in manufacturing. If the car door didn't quite fit in the chassis, you would probably see some immediate corrective action. The person making the car door would probably not be allowed to whine about how its design was better and more leading edge. It is almost unbelievable that we seem perfectly willing to tolerate this kind of situation in information systems.

The recent concept of "reengineering" is to work around the problems caused by the division of labor by putting people back together in process-driven organizations. This can solve some of the integration problems, but you can't have everyone working for one boss and, at some point, some kind of division of labor is necessary. The glue to integrate the enterprise across the disconnects that are naturally a part of the division of labor is information. We can integrate information more easily than we can integrate the organization chart.

We take standards so much for granted that it is hard to imagine what the world was like when they didn't exist. Imagine, if there were still no standard units of measure? Albeit, in North America there are still really two standard units of measure, the yard and metric system. However, at least we can translate, another benefit of standards. Although most of the modern standards we utilize today were created in the last few centuries, in some cases their building blocks come from antiquity. Back on the bus.

2.3.1   Ancient Standards as Building Blocks to Modern Standards

In ancient times, the cubit was the original unit of measure and was based on the length of a man's forearm. As you might guess, it wasn't a particularly precise unit of measure, and who knows what the women did when they needed to measure something.

Eventually, some more workable standards were set, although certainly ancient Egyptian cultural bias shows up in their decision to fix the cubit of a man at 17.72 inches and the cubit of a king at 20.62 inches. Some other important building blocks were created when the Greeks introduced the standard foot (based on Hercules' foot or so the story goes) and the Romans eventually added the idea of a mile based upon one thousand paces.[1]

Standards are not always perfect in the beginning. Typically, as standards increase in importance, they affect a larger community, and therefore their definitions get more precise as a broader viewpoint is utilized. As an example, eventually the metric system was introduced as the international standard unit of measure, and the meter is now defined as "the distance traveled by light in a vacuum during one 299,792,458th of a second." However, I don't think light travels that fast in my vacuum, so that definition may still need more precision. Are they talking a Sears or a Hoover? Is the bag full or empty? Those are pretty key questions in my mind.

Incidentally, the second is now defined as "the duration of 9,192,631,770 periods of the radiation corresponding to the transition between the two hyperfine levels of the ground state of the cesium-133 atom."[2] And we can't even agree on a standard way to identify customers across two databases.

2.3.2 War Drives New Standards

Standards bodies in the United States emerged from the private sector even though most other countries took a government approach to standards right up front. Standards became very practical solutions to urgent problems. In many cases, war provided the impetus for standards. Standard clothing sizes were introduced during the Civil War to get thousands of men in uniforms more efficiently. As the war dragged on, scarcity of materials caused even more standardization. Parts for guns needed to be interchangeable in the field. As manufacturers were no longer able to produce all parts themselves, secondary suppliers demanded standards so their parts could work equally well.

2.3.3 Large Business Opportunities Drive New Standards

When you define your enterprise information standards, one of the more difficult arguments you will run into is the magnitude of effort required to rework systems to conform. This is again another reason why business leadership is required. In a forty-eight-hour period during April

1. Achsah Nesmith, "A Long Arduous March Toward Standardization," *Smithsonian Magazine*, March 1985: 176.

2. Nesmith, p. 192.

1886, eleven thousand miles of rail between the South and the North, tracks that were incompatible during the Civil War, were converted to a standard width[3]. If that could be done, surely we can implement some information standards in your company. The railroad conversion didn't happen because a standards body came along and insisted that tracks conform. There was significant business opportunity at stake. It takes business leadership to see the opportunities that standards can provide in the enterprise, and it takes business leadership to make that kind of commitment.

Contrary to some arguments, standards do not wipe out competition and free enterprise. In 1916, Ben Tarbutton, the owner of a small, three-mile-long railway between Sandersville and Tennille, Georgia, wrote to the president of the much larger Pennsylvania Railroad offering to exchange rider passes between lines. The northerner refused the southerner, arrogantly suggesting that the Pennsylvania owned thousands of miles of track to his three. His reply indicates the importance that standards play to free enterprise. "It is true that my railroad may not be as long as yours," he replied, "but it, sir, is just as wide."[4]

2.4 TECHNOLOGY INDUSTRY STANDARDS

A more recent example of standards driven by business opportunity is in the computer industry. As the market for computers expanded, it attracted more vendors. Previous to the development of networking standards, customers were held as virtual hostages to a single vendor's product line. It was so difficult to connect disparate vendor hardware that most companies took the easier route of buying from only one primary vendor, although that didn't always protect them from autonomous divisions of the same vendor. Vendors who were established as the first computer supplier for a customer had a large advantage over any competition and reduced business opportunities for other vendors within that company. When customers were no longer willing to be held hostage to a single vendor, the key vendors created consortiums to define and manage networking and operating system standards. Those vendors that quickly implemented these types of industry standards have been the most successful in sustaining growth and profits. Computer vendors who have been reluctant to give up their lucrative but proprietary approaches have paid the price in business opportunity in the past few years.

3. Nesmith, p. 182.
4. Nesmith, p. 177.

2.5 NOT EVERYTHING BECOMES A STANDARD

As opposed to mass production, craftspeople pride themselves on uniqueness. The idea of standards for craftspeople isn't really applicable. There are in fact processes in some companies that need to remain as an art. If you want to position your business processes as crafts that provide unique results each time they occur, standards are not important and in fact will get in the artist's way. But perhaps order entry and inventory management are not crafts.

It is important to note that clearly not all features of a new technology become standard. Only those features that hinder industry growth or cause customer dissatisfaction because of vendor uniqueness evolve into standards. A commentary in *Computerworld* by George Shaffner, former chief operating officer of X/Open Company, one of those industry consortiums mentioned before, advocates the same idea.

> Let's change the definition to "Open systems are products in which low-value differentiation has been voluntarily eliminated by consensus." There are several important implications in this definition. They include the following:
> - Only low-value differentiation has been eliminated. This lets vendors continue to invest in high-value product features with the prospect of reasonable return on investment.
> - When the value of portability or interoperability (commonality) exceeds the value of differentiation (uniqueness), then the feature should be deemed as having low value and is a candidate for standardization."[5]

Therefore "customer-useful" differentiating features will not tend to evolve into standards. You may want to be able to choose the color of your car, but you want it to have a standard wheel size so you can buy your tires at that discount store along with that two-gallon jar of mayonnaise. As we design the enterprise information architecture, you will see that not everything becomes a standard. It is only where interoperability is important that standards become required.

As a person who drives rental cars very often, I could appreciate a stand-up comedian who warned his audience to watch out for rental cars on the highway during a rainstorm since the driver probably hasn't found the wipers yet. It would be interesting to see what additional car features would evolve into standards if all automobile customers regu-

5. "Redefining Open Systems," July 4, 1994: 37.

larly drove a different car every day. It might no longer be a useful differentiating feature to have wiper switches in different places. Note that it would be new customer demand that would drive the need for additional standards. I vote for a standard location for wipers in rental cars. You can put the headlight switch anywhere you want because I usually have at least a little advance notice of sunset, although, come to think of it, that solar eclipse did cause a problem.

Standards that evolve to address one roadblock to industry growth may uncover the next set of roadblocks. The computer industry is a good case in point here. Once hardware interconnectivity standards emerged, it became apparent that we had to deal with software interconnectivity, hence all that object linking and embedding (OLE) and OpenDoc stuff that hasn't sorted itself out yet. It is important to understand that these vendor standards do not address information and process standards in your enterprise, only the technology highway to enable interconnectivity.

For any newly emerging industry, there is a cycle that begins with proprietary and competing approaches, followed by customer uncertainty and confusion over these proprietary approaches. This leads to active development of standards, followed by a more stable period leaving only customer-useful differentiating features between vendors. The computer hardware and networking industry is in the active standards phase. The commercial software industry is in the uncertainty and confusion phase. At least within our own enterprise, we need to move into the phase of active standards development for information and processes in the enterprise.

2.6 DANGER DRIVES ADDITIONAL STANDARDS

Sometimes disasters are the catalyst for standards. The expansion of steam power caused 1,400 explosions per year because of the lack of boiler standards. The Baltimore fire demolished seventy city blocks because other fire companies rushing to help from other cities couldn't link their hoses to the Baltimore hydrants.[6]

The lack of electrical standards caused the creation of the U.S. National Bureau of Standards in 1901. Interestingly enough, a small fire at the National Bureau of Standards in 1904 caused a little commotion. When some dry leaves caught fire on the premises of the National

6. Nesmith, pp. 185–6.

Bureau of Standards, an employee quickly gathered up a bunch of hoses only to find that the hose threads were incompatible and could not be coupled.[7] I bet that was a topic on the next morning's agenda. In this case, the employee resorted to stamping it out just as we do in the enterprise when we find gaps between critical processes and information caused by a lack of standards.

2.7 STANDARDS IN INFORMATION ARCHITECTURES

War, danger, significant business opportunities—these have always been the breeding ground for standards. Does this sound like the environment your company is competing in? Standards that are provided by an enterprise information architecture will allow you to simplify, streamline, and in essence become a lean, mean, fighting machine in the war of business competition. In addition, it will allow you to integrate information and intelligence across your enterprise to help you find new business opportunities. Companies that implement enterprise information architectures first will be very difficult to compete with. They will have a double-edged sword. A streamlined, cost-efficient company with incredible information intelligence competing against bloated companies full of redundancy and lacking information for decision support will not be a pretty sight (unless you're the streamlined company).

2.7.1 Resistance to Standards Is Natural

Unfortunately, standards don't excite many people. It's hard work to create standards and it's not very glamorous. Plato provided some of the world's first discourses around the concept of information standards and, as Nietzsche said, "Plato is a bore."

Standards are also, by nature, a compromise. Someone, somewhere, will always be unhappy with some existing standard. I'm sure there were a lot of disagreements about the best diameter for a hose coupler, but at some point compromise was reached in the interest of coupling hoses and putting the fires out. Some of the resistance to standards in your enterprise will come from people in your company who aren't very good team players. They typically won't go along with any standard that wasn't their idea. There's not a lot you can do about this other than to force them to conform or let them come up with the standards. One of the earlier units of measure, the Saxon yard, was based on a man's girth. This

---

7. *Global Standards: Building Blocks for the Future*, the U.S. Congress, Office of Technology Assessment, 1992: 43.

was obviously not a very effective measure, although I have since noticed that thirty-six-inch Levis are a pretty popular size. So, good old Henry the First decreed a yard would henceforth equal the length of his own arm[8]. Oh well, it least it was a standard. You will probably run into a few Henrys when you are setting standards in your company.

Even though some resistance to standards comes from very egocentric individuals, the majority of the resistance will be from people who assume that information architectures and their standards will eliminate their jobs or at least reduce the creative aspects of their job. These are pretty threatening thoughts. A lot of other excuses will be given, but these are the underlying causes for most of the resistance against an enterprise architecture. These perceptions have to be brought out into the open and addressed. If people feel their job would be eliminated or they would be relegated to mundane tasks, it is only natural for them to resist. Certainly, we can't expect anyone to willingly volunteer for this.

From history we learn that the exact opposite happens. Standards and control in the right places can free engineers, artists, and scientists from tedium and allow them to increase the creative aspects of their jobs in addition to fueling industry growth and employment. These are the points that need to be used to gain and maintain support for the architecture throughout the company.

Most arguments for architectures tend to focus on the benefits to the overall company. Most employees, other than perhaps the president of the company, have a hard time relating to such global benefits. This type of sales pitch sets most architecture projects up for grassroots sabotage. The architecture will be considered more of a policing function than a valued infrastructure.

2.7.2 Standards Fuel Growth and Create Jobs

The maturity of any new industry eventually requires standards to facilitate widespread acceptance and provide the growth necessary to sustain it as a viable industry. In any technology's infancy, standards can severely limit development since competing proprietary implementations of the technology fuel the fundamental development of the technology itself. However, remember that one driving factor of standards is business opportunity. Standards emerge as necessary when uncertainty in the customer community over proprietary approaches slows down

8. Nesmith, p. 178.

industry growth, forcing vendors to work together to identify and support industry standards.

The lessons of history continue to be useful. In the early stages of the automobile, the cost and the lack of an infrastructure prohibited widespread use. As costs came down and technology improved, increased usage of automobiles led to chaos on roadways that were shared with horse-drawn carriages, wagons, and people on foot. The need for a controlled infrastructure for automobiles emerged out of necessity. Standards were set such as highway numbering systems, standard road signs and road widths, driving rules, gas and brake pedal positions, and on and on. The automobile industry experienced explosive growth as the roadblocks to widespread use were eliminated through standardization. Imagine if none of these standards had ever been put in place. Certainly, the automobile would not be a very effective way to get around, and the automobile industry would not be anywhere near the size it is today.

There is the potential loss of certain types of jobs with standardization. One of the first attempts at railroad standardization in the United States in 1853 resulted in a bloody riot. The source of all this conflict was that workers in some towns were going to lose jobs previously needed to unload, jack up, change wheels, and reload rail cars traveling on incompatible railways.[9] However, the reality was that overall jobs increased because of the expansion of rail travel enabled by standards.

In the enterprise, you will run into the same situation. You may in fact have to decrease employment in "gap management" jobs, jobs created because there were incompatible systems and processes. You will have to address the concerns of the people in these jobs because they are the largest potential saboteurs for a coordinated information architecture. If you don't address these concerns, you may find yourself in a bloody riot if you're not careful. Even though you could opt to downsize through the elimination of redundancy provided by an architected approach, it is not a good idea. Primarily this is because you will find very quickly that you need those people now that the architecture allows you to easily and inexpensively automate in areas where you have only dreamed of doing so.

The second reason not to use the architecture effort to reduce employment is that it will be hard to maintain support for a coordinated approach if people feel it is primarily a downsizing effort. If your goal is to reduce information systems employment, a potential option is to

9. Nesmith, p. 178.

migrate gap management positions to newly available positions but let normal attrition shrink the workforce over time. However, if you do reduce your information systems headcount, those people will be sucked into the expanded computer industry once standards become the norm in information systems architectures.

2.7.3 Standards Increase Creativity

Andrew Grove, CEO of Intel, coined the term "industrial democracy" and credits it with increasing both creative innovation and industry growth. He gives the example of how ski boots work with any binding and any binding works with any ski—the sporting equipment industry's version of standards. He credits these standards with permitting innovation to take place independently in boots, bindings, and skis. He also indicates that industry growth is maximized, fueling fast paced, technological breakthroughs enabled by the competitor independence provided by standards.[10]

The personal computer industry is an interesting case in point. Prior to PC hardware standards and a de facto operating system standard from Microsoft, very few PC software vendors were successful in sustaining growth and profits because vendors either had to narrow their offering down to a single PC operating system or get bogged down in maintaining multiple versions of their software packages. Software vendors were very dependent on hardware vendors and operating system vendors. With the emergence of standards, innovation can be provided independently from PC hardware vendors, PC software vendors, and PC operating system vendors such as Microsoft. There are now thousands of successful and profitable software vendors lending creative solutions to enterprises.

However, it will be interesting to see if vendor-owned de facto industry standards such as Windows can survive in free enterprise. Some of us who work in the computer industry may think that PCs are a common household item. However, at this point, only about 30 percent of homes in the United States and 10 percent of homes in other countries have personal computers.[11] Of the remaining 70 percent of Americans who don't yet have PCs in their homes, about 70 percent of those don't think they ever will, at least at this point.[12] Obviously PCs are not considered main-

10. Stratford Sherman, "How Intel Makes Spending Pay Off," *Fortune Magazine*, February 22, 1993: 57.

11. John Swenson, "Microsoft Warns of 'Risky' Future," *Journal American*, October 29, 1994: C1.

12. Tom Murphy, "Information Superhighway? Most Americans don't know what it is," *Journal American*, November 5, 1994: A8.

stream yet. As PCs become mainstream like a television or telephone, user demand for ease of use will require standardization in many areas, and it will be a miracle if vendors allow just one of their peers to supply it. In the summary findings of U.S. Office of Technology Assessment's 1992 publication, "Global Standards, Building Blocks for the Future," the importance of establishing democratic standards is discussed. "How standards are set is a matter of some concern because the economic and social stakes in standards are so large. The standards development process must be fair to prevent any single interest from dictating the outcome."

2.8 THE DEMAND FOR STANDARDS COMES FROM THE CUSTOMER BASE

As I've said before, the demand for standards usually does not come from either internal or external proprietors of any technology. It comes from the users and customers of the technology who experience the confusion caused by the lack of standards. Today, most business managers don't understand what standards could do for them and therefore aren't demanding them. Once they understand how standards provided by an enterprise information architecture will streamline the enterprise and provide integrated information, watch out.

This means that the demand for standards will probably not come from your internal information systems departments, all of which have their own proprietary approaches to protect. Remember that this is a historical pattern. We've already discussed that it is not always in a proprietor's best interest to agree on standards since in the early stages of a technology, proprietors compete against each other on the relative merit of their approach. However, customers eventually exercise their purchasing power. Can you imagine anyone buying an American appliance that would not plug into a home's already existing wiring (Figure 2–1)?

111
Volts?

Figure 2–1
Technology without standards

No one would purchase such an appliance today. It is interesting to note that, once in place, standards become sort of a "why didn't we think of this a long time ago?" type of thing. They are such an obvious solution to complexity that you wonder why they don't happen with much less conflict. The conflict over standards is most likely due to the nature of free competition, democracy, and our western culture of individualism. Since those are all pretty good things, we will just have to deal with the conflict side of setting standards. Again, you see why strong leadership to manage conflict in the standard-setting process in the enterprise is so critical.

Just like the coupling of fire hoses, there has always been a similar need for information interconnectivity within the enterprise. It has become more obvious now as business managers are reengineering their processes. I must admit that I have a hard time with the word reengineering since it implies that you engineered in the first place. An enterprise information architecture really is the first engineered approach we have ever taken to information processing. The concept of business process reengineering (BPR) requires that core business processes appear seamless across organizational boundaries. This will also demand that the applications and databases that support these processes be interconnected, requiring standards and an architectural framework. Business process reengineering cannot occur without a standards-based information systems architecture.

Internal information systems organizations are basically vendors of proprietary approaches to software and database development within the enterprise. If we follow the historical pattern, the demand for standards will come not from the internal or external proprietors of technology, but from the business community tired of finding huge system roadblocks to enterprise process reengineering—another reason for business leadership.

Marketing textbooks describe a product life cycle that includes the phases of introduction, growth, maturity, and decline. The peak at maturity occurs as the masses accept the product. Those peaks are coincidental to the implementation of standards that provide the infrastructure to allow mass usage. The standards increasingly demanded by the business and provided by the information architecture will spark creative and interesting applications of technology in areas that have always been beyond the horizon to information systems organizations bogged down with tedious interconnectivity issues. A chapter in a book by Robert Brady appropriately titled "Balance between Order and Innovation" discusses the stages of product development as "First, discovery in pure science research; second, applied science; third, invention; fourth, industrial research; fifth, industrial application; sixth, **standardization;** and seventh, mass production."[13] The commercial information systems industry needs, as Brady suggests, to balance between order (standards) and innovation.

In this brave new world of enterprise information architectures, internal information systems organizations will divide into groups of engineers who design the architecture and standards for enterprise information and groups of software artists freed up to create user interfaces into this "info-structure" for the masses. Standards will also provide guidance and selection criteria for third-party applications so they can fit into the architecture. Most astute third parties have seen this trend and are already able to use customizing technology to adapt to an enterprise's data or technology standards. There will be a significant increase in information systems employment as the ability to bring technology to the masses is provided through standards. For these reasons, information systems organizations should be heartily embracing the idea of an enterprise information architecture.

Much like the understated importance of underground utilities and highways, an enterprise information architecture will eventually become a de facto, accepted, and unquestioned part of the enterprise infrastructure. The idea of building a system without conforming to the enterprise architecture will be considered naive and silly, much like suggesting that a car be designed a foot wider than the standard lane size. From cacophony to symphony. An impromptu drum solo will no longer be allowed in the middle of the enterprise dance of the sugar plum fairy.

2.9 WHAT THE FUTURE HOLDS

The Manifest Destiny was the belief that it was inevitable for the United States to expand all the way to the Pacific Coast. With the same sense of confidence, it is inevitable that the wave of standards encompassing the computer hardware industry will expand to the commercial software industry. It is inevitable that you will eventually buy your software components at a retail outlet and plug them into your architecture like installing a new appliance in your kitchen. You will buy an order processing module from vendor A and a distribution module from vendor B and they will interoperate. A year or maybe even a few months later, you'll

13. *Organization, Automation, and Society: The Scientific Revolution in Industry,* 1961.

replace your distribution module with something from vendor C because it is better or faster. It is inevitable that this will happen; it is your manifest destiny.

Interoperability will significantly increase customer choice. The number of software suppliers entering the market will explode because the barriers to entry will disappear. Suppliers will be forced to compete on price, service, quality, and innovation within the constraints of interoperability in this commodities market. They will not necessarily do it willingly.

This manifest destiny is up to you, the business manager. It will happen only when **you** demand that software interoperate and no sooner. Software developers, both yours and theirs, will probably not argue for interoperability. The largest software vendors today are large because they have proprietary approaches that integrate their modules and no one else's. It will not be in their best short-term interest to interoperate with other, smaller software vendors.

However, the commercial software interoperability revolution is under way. This revolution is as big as the mathematics revolution that snowballed through a series of discoveries by people like Galileo, Descartes, and Newton.

> In mathematics it is new ways of looking at old things that seem to be the most prolific sources of far-reaching discoveries. A particular fact may have been known for centuries, and it may have been sterile or of only minor interest all that time, when suddenly some original mind glimpses it from a new angle and perceives the gateway to an empire. What the first flash of intuition sees may take years or even centuries to open up and explore completely, but once a start in the right direction is made, discovery and development go forward at an ever-increasing speed."[14]

Put your seatbelts on, the speed is picking up. Small starts in the right direction have already occurred. Look for those small articles hidden on the back page of computer publications. "The oil industry took a giant step last week toward leveraging open systems to cut information technology costs. Now at the end of a three month long, $500,000 industry pilot project, the Petrotechnical Open Software Corp. will ask 150 software vendors to port their applications to a common data model and set of open systems standards. Seven of the world's largest oil firms—

14. Eric Temple Bell, *Mathematics, Queen and Servant of Science*, 1951, p. 94.

such as BP Exploration, Arco Oil and Gas Co., Mobil Oil Corp and Shell Oil Co, U.S. backed the pilot." This article by Jean Bozman appeared in the April 11, 1994, edition of *Computerworld* (p.1) and received little attention.

Back in 1961, Brady was discussing the snowball effect of standards in industry. "As a consequence, scarcely have standards been developed for corporate use when the need for conferences arises for the development of standards of mutual interest to entire industries or congeries of industries. Sale of products on widening and more distant markets adds further pressure for expansion of standards." (p. 141)

It will take customer consortiums like the Petrotechnical Open Software Corporation to really get the commercial software standards ball rolling. One might envision consortiums by major industry since the information and processes necessary for the oil industry are quite different from those of the wholesale/retail distribution industry for example. These consortiums will be driven by leaders in each industry. They will start in areas where cooperation is of benefit to these leaders. For example, the Petrotechnical Open Software Corporation is focused on the oil exploration area where all companies drilling in the same area share the same risks. A few success stories will lead to the evaluation in other areas even in industries where competition among leaders is fierce.

Commercial computing will never reach its potential without a rational system of information processing standards both within the enterprise and between enterprises. Listen to Robert Brady again: "Almost every main aspect of the scientific revolution in industry reveals the importance and the implications of a rational system of standards. It may readily be shown that the extent to which any economy is enabled to make the fullest and most effective use of the newer mass-output methods depends, more clearly than upon any other single technical factor, upon the nature, comprehensiveness, and general viability of its system of standards." (p. 108)

The Business Approach to Enterprise Information Architecture Design

The dictionary defines an architect as one who builds structures, especially habitable ones. We would be hard pressed to define the jumbled network of current systems in most enterprises as architectures under this definition. Architecture implies a planned and controlled approach, not the reactive style heavily utilized by my son Jesse when he builds a fort with his friends or by software developers reacting to the latest user request by haphazardly plugging a new application into the mass of systems already in the enterprise.

3.1 WHAT IS AN ARCHITECTURE?

Architecture is, once again, an ancient field of study. Back on the bus.

Most of us think of architecture as a discipline that is relevant only to building physical structures like office buildings. However, the planning concepts that separate architecture from construction are the same when designing an enterprise information architecture. In a book entitled *Architecture, A Short History*, a summary of the fundamental ancient contributions to the field of architecture indicates the importance of its planning component.

> These ancient civilizations made three principal contributions to the development of architecture. One was the perfection of two structural systems, the post and lintel and the arch, and their use as decorative as well as structural elements. Another was a multitude of decorative forms and patterns, many of which passed into the architectural heri-

tage of Western Civilization and are still in use today. The third was the concept of orderly planning.... The most important of these contributions is perhaps the last, for plan is fundamental in architecture.[1]

You may have heard of the famous Code of Hammurabi. Hammurabi was the king of Babylon in 1750 B.C. He ruled during what was considered to be the Golden Age of Babylon where he provided a very fair, but highly coordinated government. The idea of a unified government was a novel concept back then. At that time, Mesopotamia was made up of small scattered kingdoms and tribes who disagreed on just about everything, including some pretty basic stuff like the calendar. (Sound like your company?)

Hammurabi's famous code was a body of law that was drawn up over four thousand years ago and included such forward-thinking ideas like the right to a fair trial. It also included this important rule for architects: "If a builder constructed a house, but did not make his work strong, with the result that the house which he built collapsed and so has caused the death of the owner of the house, that builder shall be put to death."[2] In the time of Hammurabi, enterprise information architectures would have been pretty darn good.

3.2 ENTERPRISE INFORMATION ARCHITECTURES— THE HORIZONTAL APPROACH

Using the ancient concept of architecture as a planned approach to building something, the enterprise information systems architecture framework developed a decade ago by John Zachman provides the best approach for designing an enterprise information architecture. An enterprise information architecture allows integration and coordination across the enterprise. Integration and coordination always require a shift away from a vertical or proprietary approach to a horizontal approach that cuts across the organization. Zachman's architectural framework provided for a fundamental shift from the previous vertical information system development paradigm to a coordinated or planned approach using a horizontal paradigm. Like all vertical to horizontal shifts, it is a radical shift. Unfortunately, even though the Zachman framework is over a decade old, this paradigm shift for information systems development has not even begun in most enterprises.

1. Joseph Watterson, 1968, p. 21.
2. Albert Champdor, *Babylon*, 1958, p. 46.

However, the radical shift from vertical to horizontal is starting elsewhere in the enterprise and is the same approach underlying business process reengineering. John A. Byrne's cover story in the December 20, 1993, *Business Week,* entitled "The Horizontal Corporation," discusses some of the benefits of this shift. "As DuPont's Terry Ennis puts it: 'Our goal is to get everyone focused on the business as a system in which the functions are seamless.' DuPont executives are trying to do away with what Ennis calls the 'disconnects' and 'hand-offs' that are so common between functions and departments. 'Every time you have an organizational boundary, you get the potential for a disconnect,' Ennis says. 'The bigger the organization, the bigger the functions and the more disconnects you get.'"

3.3 A VERTICAL APPROACH TO SYSTEMS DEVELOPMENT ENCOURAGES DISCONNECTS IN THE ENTERPRISE

The vertical approach to information systems development creates the same disconnects as a vertical approach to organizations. It was encouraged by the need to have systems development teams align more closely with a set of users. However, these vertically aligned information systems organizations are peaked to satisfy small groups of individual contributors, not business executives interested in streamlining and integrating the enterprise. Author Larry Runge also concurs with this situation. "The information technology psyche began at a department level or lower, rather than at a business or enterprise level. As a result, systems design became very department-dependent, often to the point at which expenditures and activities were optimized to the benefit of the department and the detriment of the enterprise."[3]

Today's heavy emphasis on end-user satisfaction continues to encourage a departmental myopia, creating vertical systems with their own proprietary data, software, and technology components. Each system is peaked for productivity within a department, not the enterprise. A good example of this myopic view is that a traditional metric for user satisfaction is screen response time. Perhaps the transaction that the department cares about, such as invoicing, occurs in less than a second. What is not so obvious is that this transaction is part of a larger company-wide process, in this case order fulfillment. If you look at the whole business process, there may be hundreds of screens in many sys-

3. *Computerworld,* October 24, 1994: 113.

tems, even though each one has been carefully tweaked to take only seconds. You add the redundancy, complexity, and disconnects between departmental systems to the sum of the processing time of each of those single screens, and you don't get a streamlined and productive business process.

Peter Drucker had the same opinion about small units of work versus the whole process.

> Everybody these last few years has been talking productivity. That greater productivity—better utilization of resource—is both the key to the high standard of living and the result of business activity is not news. But we actually know very little about productivity: we are indeed not yet able to measure it. Productivity means that balance between all factors of production that will give the greatest output for the smallest effort. This is quite a different thing from productivity per worker or per hour of work; it is at best distantly and vaguely reflected in these traditional standards.[4]

3.3.1 The No-Win Teeter-Totter

A vertical approach places information technology managers on a teeter-totter. On one side of the teeter-totter is individual user satisfaction. The lowliest administrative employee in the company can complain about the screen design in an application and the information systems manager hears about it. So they run down that side of the teeter-totter to try to fix it. The industry tries to help by inventing better methodologies to get even more individual user focused, such as joint application design (JAD) or rapid application design (RAD) approaches. None of these approaches are a bad idea. However, since the information systems community is busy trying to make all the individual users happy, there is no one focused on the cross-departmental needs. Therefore, the information system needs of middle- to upper-level business managers, whose responsibilities span departments, are ignored. So they start complaining about their situation, and the information systems manager has to run down that side of the teeter-totter.

It's exhausting trying to balance between individual user and cross-functional management's needs. It's no wonder that there is a high turnover in Chief Information Officer (CIO) positions. An enterprise information architecture provides a better way to balance these competing needs (Figure 3–1).

4. *The Practice of Management*, 1954, p. 41.

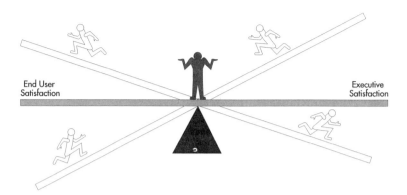

Figure 3–1
Balancing competing needs within the enterprise

3.3.2 A Vertical Approach to Systems Development Encourages Monolithic Systems

Another significant danger to a vertical information systems approach is that it created those monolithic legacy systems that are so difficult to replace. They are difficult to replace because the vertical approach to systems development tends to result in mega-applications with huge amounts of custom code. Why do they tend to get so huge?

They didn't start that way—megasystems would be impossible to write in any single system release cycle. These mega-applications have become huge over long periods of time, in some cases decades. The vertical approach encourages you to build a departmental application that attempts to automate everything the department needs to do. But most departments have overlapping data and processes with other departments in the enterprise. Instead of linking to other departments' data or software to accomplish a task, many departmental systems are continually enhanced to encroach on data and software that already exist in other information systems. Therefore the application gets bigger and bigger over the years, and software and data redundancy gets worse and worse in the enterprise.

As an example of the historically vertical approach in information systems, both marketing and order processing departments typically end up with their own customer databases since they both need access to that type of information. A horizontal approach, the Zachman approach, would design a single set of customer data that is shared between these two departments. (It will likely be more than one physical database in a large company, but it would be treated logically as one set of data.)

Some legacy applications have had development cycles of twenty years or more. It is virtually impossible to replace them with another vertical system encompassing the same functionality in any reasonable timeframe. This explains the extremely high failure rate of legacy system replacement projects. The horizontal approach taken when building an architecture breaks those monolithic systems into a more component-oriented architecture where components can be replaced in reasonable timeframes. This is what enables the insertion of new technology into the enterprise quickly and efficiently.

With the horizontal approach used in building an architecture, you design applications around processes, not departments. This may mean that a department might have to use more than one application to get its job done. Unfortunately, most users think they should have a single application to get their jobs done and are uncomfortable with the idea of using multiple applications—probably remembering the days of needing two terminals on the desk. However, the reality is that where users work with a single application, it is always two releases behind where it needs to be since the department it supports is ever changing.

The horizontal approach buffers the departmental users from organizational changes. When a department reorganizes, its new processes are automated by selecting from component applications that are either already available in the architecture or more easily created because they are not that large. It's important to note that we are not talking about enterprise-wide technology consistency between components. These components can be **any** technology, including good old-fashioned terminal-to-host applications. Where you have a chance to replace legacy systems and make them component oriented, new technologies will help hide the boundaries between components. One of the very active R&D areas in the computer industry is in the area of application linking. OLE, Open-Doc, and other application-linking technologies are in the process of sorting themselves out, and at some point a standard will emerge.

To understand this move from vertical to horizontal and how it creates a component-oriented architecture, think of processes as crayons and departmental applications as packaging. You are holding blue, green, and red (processes) which are shrink-wrapped together into a single package (departmental application). I am holding yellow, black, and purple in a single package. Now we reorganize; I need blue, green, and purple and you need yellow, black, and red. We both have to tear our packages apart, swap colors, and package them back together—in other words rewrite both applications. If we were holding individual colors, we would just be able to swap the purple and red and be done. In an architected environment, software components will get replaced because of new technology or a reengineered process, not because of a reorganization. In other words, we may buy a new red crayon when the old one wears out. With this approach, it is extremely important to get the components right in the first place. In the previous example, if I needed the color orange, I would have needed part of red and part of yellow. How to break the architecture down into the right components is addressed in the methodology of designing an enterprise information architecture.

3.4 ADVANTAGE OF ZACHMAN'S HORIZONTAL APPROACH

An enterprise information architecture provides a component orientation that enables the movement to smaller, more easily upgradeable systems. The architecture defines the natural boundaries between components. These components are intended to meet the individual users' needs on the one side of the teeter-totter. The architecture also defines which components need to integrate with each other and how. The integration between components meets cross-functional management needs on the other side of the teeter-totter (Figure 3–2).

This component orientation of an enterprise information architecture breaks the architecture into information systems. Most of us think that the term "information system" is synonymous with application, but it was never intended to have such a narrow meaning since the word *system* means an assembly of things that form a unified whole. "Information system" in the context of an architecture means a set of clients or applications that are related because they share similar data. The enterprise information architecture defines where the natural boundaries are

Figure 3–2
User needs and cross-functional management needs in balance

between these information systems. The information systems are the "rooms" of the enterprise information system architecture. These boundaries are our first set of architecture standards. Once these natural boundaries are set, system developers must conform to them.

These very succinct information system boundaries provide the framework to prevent a developer from tacking on redundant data or software that can be better found in another part of the architecture in another information system. If a systems developer has a data or process need outside the preestablished boundary of an information system, they are required by the architecture to access another information system rather than create redundancy. Of course, standards to allow these linkages between information systems are critical, much like ensuring that state highways can link together to create an interstate highway.

As an example of how this horizontal approach works, if the developer of an order processing information system needs to access information about potential customers or prospects, he or she would most likely be required by the architecture to access the marketing information system. The reason for this is that most architectures define a set of marketing-oriented processes that share primarily prospect/customer-oriented data, where order-management-oriented processes share primarily order-oriented data. Even though the order management information system requires access to prospect data, the architecture does not allow it to be created within its boundaries.

The precise information system boundaries that an architecture defines makes the overall architecture component oriented. This prevents the creation of mega-applications. The architecture will also identify how developers should break legacy application replacement projects down into more manageable projects. Legacy applications most likely span more than one information system using our new definition. To replace the legacy system, you strip off what belongs in other information systems as separate projects.

All new systems become legacy systems at some point. Once you have migrated to the new information system boundaries, each new individual information system can more easily be replaced with another information system utilizing new technology but with the exact same boundaries. The boundaries of each information system in an architected environment never change, just the particular technology or process methodology. Think of it as getting to the point where you have to remodel only a single room when replacing a system, not tear down the whole house. This is one of the key advantages of an architecture.

Zachman's framework provides the necessary detailed, complete, and robust view of the enterprise information architecture (Figure 3–3). It provides for six increasingly detailed levels or views of all three architectures—data, process, and technology. Think of this as providing all views of a home from the artist's drawing, through the blueprints, and down to the individual contractor's plans for brickwork or plumbing.

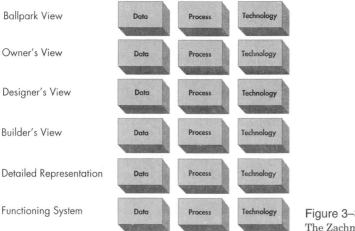

Figure 3–3
The Zachman framework

3.5 THE BUSINESS VIEWS OF ENTERPRISE INFORMATION ARCHITECTURES

Most of the strategic business breakthroughs from this approach are found at the top rows or views of the Zachman framework. These top two rows are business management views of the architecture and have nothing to do with technology. The lower levels of the architecture have to do with building actual applications and databases. However, this author will focus only on the top two rows of the Zachman framework and only on the data and process architectures of those rows (Figure 3–4).

There are three primary reasons for this focus.

1. The first reason for focusing on the business views is that, like any undertaking, having a plan is the only way to ensure success unless you want to plan on blind luck. If you don't have a solid plan, no amount of detailed tactical deployment will fix the problem. Most architectural efforts skim through the higher-level views and spend months and years mired in the more technical detailed views of the architecture. We will emphasize the higher-

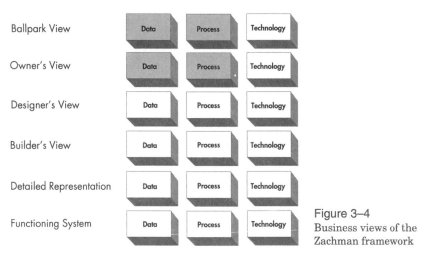

Ballpark View

Owner's View

Designer's View

Builder's View

Detailed Representation

Functioning System

Figure 3–4
Business views of the
Zachman framework

level views of the architecture since they define the strategy. The lower levels must be completed during development of any one particular component such as a new application. But they are relegated to the realm of tactical deployment where they belong.

Once the business views of the architecture are defined, individual system projects will no longer have autonomy in *what* they deploy, only *how* they deploy it. Their high-level functional boundaries or *what* should be automated in any one information system will be succinctly outlined in the business views. *How* it should be automated will not. Information Technology should still be given free rein to creatively deploy the "how" of the architecture. They have the best expertise to make the appropriate tradeoffs in the physical architecture as it evolves to meet the business views.

Most enterprises cannot afford to rebuild something akin to the interstate highway system every few years. The reality is that, even if it were affordable, it would not be possible. It is critical to get the top-level architecture right the first time because you will not get many chances to do it again.

2. The second reason for the emphasis on only the business views of the architecture is that the higher-level views of the architecture are the foundation and must stand the test of time. The lower levels of the architecture and the entire technology architecture is unstable. Enterprises should replace applications regularly as process improvements are found. Better DBMS technology

should regularly replace databases. Companies will purchase and implement new computers and networks.

Fundamental breakthroughs will continue to be made in technology. It is a mistake to assume that all legacy applications will go away. In reality, new "legacy" applications will just replace them. This should not be a depressing thought. You should expect that the lower levels of the Zachman framework will be reworked regularly, much like repainting the rooms in your home on a periodic basis to maintain your investment. The business views of the enterprise information architecture will make it easier to keep up with new technology. They provide a solid foundation to facilitate the fast and efficient rollover of both the technology architecture and the lower levels of the Zachman framework. The business views of the data and process architectures are like the fundamental design of the house, and the rest of the architecture is like the furniture and appliances that come and go. Client/ server and object-oriented applications and the next generation of new technology will come and go. That latest round of high-tech stuff that your application development team just convinced you will solve all your business problems will be obsolete in a few years. Unless you put the business views of an architecture in place to facilitate its replacement, that brand-new, high-tech application you just installed will become a low-tech albatross you can't ever seem to get rid of. Just worry about the business views of the architecture and let your contractors worry about the latest and greatest building materials.

3. The third reason for the emphasis on the business views of the architecture is that these are the only views the business community understands. In order to gain control over computing assets, the business community needs to understand the architecture that provides the structure that guides, scopes, and controls implementation utilizing internal or external contractors.

Many significant business and information systems breakthroughs can be made during the development of the business views of the enterprise information architecture. In order to discover these breakthroughs, you must have direct business management involvement including executives. If the architect takes the bus to the fifth station while developing the business views, business managers will be spared some of the tedium that usually encourages them to drop out of an architectural effort. After all, they have a business to run, airplanes to build, pension funds to manage, pulp to process into paper.

3.6 WHO IS THE ARCHITECT?

When building a home, the key players are the homeowners, the architect, and the contractors. If you take that approach and apply it to information systems, business managers are the homeowners and the information systems community is analogous to the contractors. We are missing the concept of architect in the commercial information processing industry. An architect works primarily for the homeowners; therefore the architect of an enterprise information architecture should work for business management. This architect should ideally have well-rounded line management experience and be an expert on the Zachman framework and information engineering. If that is not possible, take the business background first and educate on the other aspects through training or the use of a consultant. The lower levels of the architecture should be completed by information systems experts so that the architect does not have to have significant technical depth. Outsourcing the architectural work completely to a consultant is another choice, although knowledge of your industry and ideally your particular business is critical to success.

Most significant breakthroughs will be uncovered by someone who has a broad understanding of the enterprise vision, the competition, and the overall industry the enterprise is a part of. The architect becomes a catalyst and translator for these breakthroughs. Unfortunately, many of those people who have the broad business understanding are very difficult to get as members of the architectural team. It's the architect's job to use the bus as much as possible and involve these key business managers on the final climb. If you lose business involvement in the enterprise information architecture, you are doomed, and your best option is to halt the effort.

3.7 HOW TO BUILD AN ENTERPRISE INFORMATION ARCHITECTURE

If you were designing a home, you would first lay out the floor plan by grouping related functions and items into rooms. For example, the bathtub and shower belong in the bathroom and the stove and oven belong in the kitchen. This is not an arbitrary process. Putting the stove and shower in the same room doesn't make sense because they aren't related. The goal of the business views of the architecture is to accomplish a similar task. We will group related data and processes into "information systems," the rooms of our architecture. In both cases, we are using an information processing fundamental from antiquity. Let's get back on the bus.

3.7.1 Ancient Perspective on Information Processing

As early as 400 B.C., the ancient Greeks studied information processing in their attempts to simplify their world and understand their environment. The way the ancient Greeks approached knowledge or information is important since it is so significantly different from the relatively recent western theme of individualism. Individualism could be described as the main catalyst behind an autonomous approach to information systems found in many departments within the enterprises.

3.7.2 Bias toward Simplification

The western concept of individualism obviously has a lot going for it. However, most people may not realize that it is also the main cause of complexity in our lives. The ancient Greeks always considered things as part of something larger. Integration to the Greeks was more important than separation. Standards would have been important to the Greeks. The approach of seeing things in their larger context provides a key difference between Greek philosophy and western individualism. This critical difference created the Greeks' bias toward simplification. Placed against "the background of infinity," complexities are simplified.

Our modern, individualistic approach is exactly the opposite of simplification. "We are burdened with over-realization."[5]Although much of what the ancient Greeks pondered was knowledge about the living environment, this trend toward simplicity is a useful thing to emulate when designing the enterprise information architecture. In the area of information processing, the Greeks gave us the ability to simplify by developing classification theory.

3.7.3 Architecture Classification

The ancient concept of classification is highly related to information processing. This field of study actually began with the Greek philosophers Plato and Aristotle in the fourth century B.C. This was over 2,200 years ago. It is defined as the sorting of like objects into groups and provides the ability to simplify and comprehend. Classification theory is what you use to put the bathtub and shower in the same room. It's what

5. Edith Hamilton, *The Greek Way*, 1930, p. 332.

your children do when they learn to sort objects in kindergarten. Basically, classification is the same thing as the "new" idea of object orientation that you may have heard about from the technology community.

Some people are on to the fact that object orientation isn't new. "OOA—Object-Oriented Analysis—is based upon concepts that we first learned in kindergarten: objects and attributes, wholes and parts, classes and members. Why it has taken us so long to apply these concepts to the analysis and specification of information systems is anyone's guess."[6] Well, it has been a long time since kindergarten for most of us.

Plato's interests in classification theory revolved around the search for the eiodos or essence of things and is known as existentialism. Aristotle's interests centered around logical division. In Plato's writings, he sounds like the original information architect. At the heart of his theory was the separation of opinion and knowledge. The information architect separates departmental views or opinions of information from facts. Plato would have made a great information architect. Plato, interestingly enough, had an abhorrence for buzzwords. "Just the facts, ma'am," may possibly have originally come from Plato.

3.7.3.1 What Is the Benefit of Classification?   Some of the earliest formal writings on classification are in the fields of biology and botany.[7] Theophrastus (ca 370–285 B.C.), a student of Plato and Aristotle, was the first to document a botanical classification scheme. There are many more famous classification experts in history—Charles Darwin and Carl von Linné (real name of Carolus Linnaeus) for instance. Few of us would dispute the intelligence of these scholars. Why would they focus on such a seemingly dull subject as classification theory?

An excerpt from *An Introduction to Plant Taxonomy* by C. Jeffries gives us some indication of the importance of classification theory to the ability to effectively process information. (The field of plant taxonomy is the study of the classification of plants.)

> Classification is an activity in which we engage from the very earliest days of our lives. The ability to classify is, in fact, inborn, although we may not realize it, it is essential to the existence of every living creature. In biological history, it long antedates the appearance of humanity. The new-born duckling, for example, crouches when an object that is hawk-like in shape is passed above it, but does not react in this way

6. Peter Coad, *Object-Oriented Analysis*, 1990, p. 1.
7. Clive Stace, *Plant Taxonomy and Biosystematics*, 1989, p. 18.

to one shaped, say, like a swan or heron. From this, it is clear that the duckling has the ability to classify objects of its surroundings into at least two different kinds, those that are hawk-like and those that are not. If this seems to us a trifle naive, we must remember that it is an ability of vital importance to the duckling. (p. 2)

If you didn't know that C. Jeffries's book was about plants, you might think it was about information processing.

Classification is, in fact, a general method used by us all for dealing with information.... So by classification we can organize our knowledge of the plant kingdom into a system which stores and summarizes our information for us in a convenient manner.... Clearly, some system by which we can organize this knowledge, make generalizations and predictions, and simply reduce the sheer bulk of data with which we have to deal, is not only desirable but essential. (p. 2)

Classification then, is the attempt to identify and assign like things to groups so that they can be understood and processed more easily. It basically provides a set of standards to assist in communication and simplification. Classification theory also provides the ability to anticipate the future. As Rudolf Flesch quotes John Dewey (*Reconstruction in Philosophy*), "A classification is a repertory of weapons for attack upon the future and unknown."[8] For example, matching the characteristics of a new plant with a group or class of plants that have certain disease-curing characteristics gives us another opportunity to cure the disease.

Humans have continually expanded classification into other areas at the core of human existence: the table of elements, colors, and music, for example. Classification provides structure and control. Interestingly enough it also enhances the ability to create. Certainly, you cannot create a new musical note H, but look what you can do with the notes A through G! We must call the color red, red, and the color green, green, but has that stymied the artist?

3.7.3.2 Classification as a Matter of Survival

Classification theory comes into play as it becomes necessary to simplify or better understand something. It is not by accident that the first areas to be classified were at the bottom of the famous psychologist Maslow's[9] pyramid of

8. Rudolf Flesch, *The Art of Clear Thinking*, 1951, p. 111.
9. Abraham Harold Maslow, 1908–70, American psychologist, developed a theory of human motivation.

needs—survival. It is not a coincidence that the earliest writings on classification were in the area of botany—things to eat—or that next on the list of historical priorities was classification of rocks and minerals, things that we use to build shelters.

Classification is related to the idea of standards that we discussed earlier. For example, colors are classified by a set of standard definitions for red, blue, green, and so on. Classification theory helps us understand and simplify. In order to make the kind of productivity improvements that will be demanded in industry, we must simplify the information system architecture. We do that by using classification theory. We need to better understand our information environment in order to meet executive demands for improved decision support information. The emergence of the information highway will not only require a better understanding of a single enterprise's information environment but of all enterprises on the highway. All of this can be accomplished only by applying classification theory to automated information processing.

3.7.3.3 Additional Benefits of Classification　Classifying the architecture into like groups or information systems creates standards and has the unexpected benefit of clarifying roles and responsibilities in the organization. Much of the redundancy in the architecture is caused by overlapping processes and information. The classification of the architecture forms natural divisions of labor for creating components of the architecture.

3.7.3.4 What Classification Can't Do　A classification expert can go overboard sometimes. Much as with standards, not everything should be classified. Even Plato occasionally went a little overboard. There may be parts of your enterprise that are too difficult to understand or are artistic in nature. Those are the areas where classification theory may not be applicable; they are also the areas that are typically not automated with commercial software.

3.7.3.5 Classifying the Architecture into Information Systems　The classification process is perhaps the most critical process in developing the business views of the architecture. This classification process searches for natural boundaries between parts of the architecture, much like the rooms of a house. These rooms are the information systems we discussed earlier.

There are several reasons why classifying the architecture into information systems is so critical. The first and main reason for architectural classification is that it assists in simplification by eliminating redundancy. By removing traditional organizational separation by grouping similar data and processes across the enterprise, the architecture becomes more simplified and streamlined. If you never saw another human, you might think you were unique. The expansion of civilization eventually caused all of us humans to bump into each other, albeit with sometimes disastrous consequences. However, we are now beginning to understand that we aren't unique, that we are all humans with the same rights, even though it is certainly taking longer than it should. Most traditional organizational boundaries prevent business managers from seeing these same sorts of similarities in processes and information across the enterprise.

Another reason for architectural classification is to break down a very large problem into more manageable tasks. It provides for the component orientation of the architecture. The boundaries of these components or information systems are not arbitrary. The process of classification is unique in that it provides an approach to divide a huge task into the smallest possible problems to solve and no smaller. It is much like attempting to eat a plateful of spaghetti. If the natural break points in the architecture are not defined correctly, you will never be able to stop winding the implementation fork. A software development project that seems to be in one class of an erroneously classified architecture will continually find issues that have to be addressed in another class in order to proceed. These issues will suck you into enlarging projects until you find that you have to eat the whole plate of spaghetti in one bite, which is not only a pretty hopeless endeavor but also tends to give you indigestion. This, by the way, is the danger of defining the boundaries of an information system initiative around the potentially arbitrary scope of a reengineering effort.

Architectural classification occurs in the business views of the enterprise information architecture. Once the architecture has been classified and validated, the builders and designers of components of the architecture have a road map to follow. This framework has the added advantage of assisting in project scoping since it defines the best possible boundaries with the minimum number of tentacles into other projects. As key components of the architecture are built and put in place, follow-on components get easier and easier to implement, and eventually projects look a lot more like buying a new car, not building a new freeway.

3.8 WHAT ARE THE BENEFITS OF AN ENTERPRISE INFORMATION ARCHITECTURE?

3.8.1 It Streamlines Business Processes

A fundamental benefit of building an enterprise information architecture is the discovery and elimination of redundancy in the business processes; in effect, it can drive reengineering. This occurs because the steps to building an information architecture reveal redundancy caused by different organizational views of the same process or data. Perhaps the first computing professionals had hidden meaning in their old and abandoned title of "data processing manager." The fundamental approach to building an information architecture is to focus on data and process. It is interesting to note that newer job titles in the commercial data processing field almost always have the word "technology" in them. Technology is simply a tool set in the automation of data and processes for the enterprise. Most enterprises exist to manufacture equipment, harvest trees, or distribute goods, not implement technology.

3.8.2 It Reduces Information Systems Complexity

The framework reduces information systems complexity through the same process of identifying and eliminating redundancy in data and software. The resulting enterprise information architecture will have significantly fewer applications and databases as well as a resulting reduction in intersystem links. This simplification also leads to significantly reduced costs. Some of those recuperated costs can and should be reinvested into automation of processes that have always been just beyond the budget limit. This is what will bring technology to everyone in the enterprise.

3.8.3 It Enables Enterprise-Wide Integration through Data Sharing

The information architecture identifies where it's important to create data standards for shared data. For example, most enterprises hold a wealth of information about their customers and the marketplace, but it is locked up in hundreds of incompatible databases. The information architecture forces compatibility for shared enterprise data. This compatible information can be stripped out of operational systems, merged to provide an enterprise view, and stored in data warehouses for market research and analysis. In addition, data standards streamline the operational architecture by eliminating the need to translate or even move data between systems. A well-designed architecture not only streamlines the internal value chain, but it can provide the infrastructure necessary to link value chains between companies or allow effortless substitution of value chains such as outsourcing part of a business.

3.8.4 It Enables Faster Evolution to New Technologies

Client/server and object-oriented technology revolves around the understanding of data and the processes that create and access it. Since the enterprise information architecture is structured around data and process and not redundant organizational views of the same thing, the application of client/server and object-oriented technologies is much cleaner. It is my opinion that attempting to move to client/server and/or object-oriented design without an enterprise information architecture will result in a lot of eventual rework.

3.9 DESIGNING THE BUSINESS VIEWS OF THE ARCHITECTURE

The business views of Zachman's framework are the ballpark view and the business owner's view. The purpose of both of these views is to define the boundaries of a set of information systems that cover the needs of the enterprise. The boundaries of these information systems become our first set of architectural standards in the enterprise.

3.9.1 Level One Overview—The Ballpark View

The ballpark view of the information architecture defines high-level information needs and enterprise business functions at a global enter-

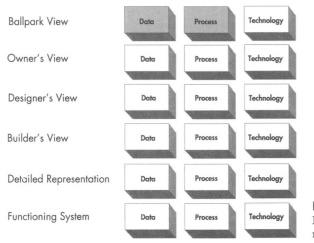

Figure 3–5
Ballpark view of the Zachman framework.

prise level. This creates a high-level definition of the enterprise information architecture through fundamental classes of data and processes.

3.9.2 Level Two Overview—The Owner's View

The second level of the architecture provides the business owner's view and defines in more detail the business functions and the information needs of the enterprise. At the second level, the fundamental classes of data and processes from the ballpark view are validated through more detailed analysis. Information engineering techniques such as data modeling and process to data affinity analysis are used in this level. Even though the business owner's view uses information engineering techniques, it is a business-owned view of the architecture. Only the business has a good understanding of its information needs at this level.

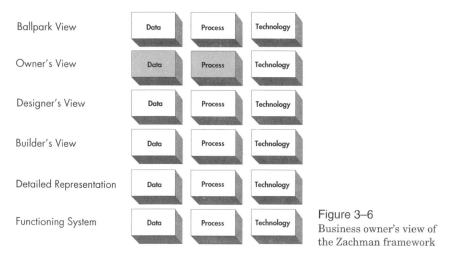

Ballpark View	Data / Process / Technology	
Owner's View	Data / Process / Technology	
Designer's View	Data / Process / Technology	
Builder's View	Data / Process / Technology	
Detailed Representation	Data / Process / Technology	
Functioning System	Data / Process / Technology	

Figure 3–6
Business owner's view of the Zachman framework

The level two architecture continues to ferret out and eliminate redundancy, leaving the cleanest, most streamlined set of data and functions possible. Picture an architect not only providing the overall drawing that meets the customer's requests but also looking for ways to reduce wiring and plumbing costs.

3.9.3 How Much Detail?

For the business views of the architecture, exhaustive analysis of information and processes in the enterprise is not required. Enough detail to test and validate the architectural classification into information systems suffices. The business view of the architecture can be completed pretty quickly, so you shouldn't have a problem maintaining business sponsorship if you do it right.

Once the business views are established, the playing field boundaries are identified for each information system. Then, each information system can be constructed with less business involvement, bringing the right expertise to bear at the right points in the development and implementation of the architecture.

3.10 ARCHITECTURAL DEPENDENCIES

The last step in completing the business view of the architecture is to determine dependencies, priorities, and migration plans. In this step, information systems are analyzed for their dependance on one another. Information systems that rely on foundation information from other information systems need to be built last. Unfortunately, almost all dependency analyses identify that the not-so-glamorous architectural components need to be built first, like a boring old reference database for products or customers that can be used by multiple information systems. However, most of these boring components provide the capability to integrate the enterprise.

It's difficult to garner enthusiasm about these fundamental projects, somewhat like trying to get a homeowner excited about the cement foundation. The message has to be conveyed to executives that the less glamorous building blocks of the enterprise information architecture are critical. Unfortunately, you have to pour concrete before it makes sense to build the master bedroom suite. You convey this message by executive involvement in the architecture. As the business managers get involved in developing the architecture, it will become more obvious why the fundamental, less glamorous building blocks are so important, and it will finally become easier to get business sponsorship for these projects.

Once the dependencies have been established, you can begin building the components of the architecture. Using an earlier analogy, you hire the best contractors you can and rely on their expertise and experience to construct the information systems within the boundaries defined in the business views of the architecture.

The Ballpark View of the Process Architecture

We begin defining the enterprise information architecture by examining the enterprise-wide business processes. The ballpark view of the process architecture identifies the key enterprise functions that run the business. Even at this level of the Zachman's framework, we are already taking a stab at classification. Think of it as sketching the general idea for a new home by making a rough draft of the floor plan (Figure 4–2). You probably don't think that you are using classification theory when you are sketching your floor plan with an architect because there are already well-established classifications for this purpose. It is an almost uncon-

Ballpark View	Data	Process	Technology
Owner's View	Data	Process	Technology
Designer's View	Data	Process	Technology
Builder's View	Data	Process	Technology
Detailed Representation	Data	Process	Technology
Functioning System	Data	Process	Technology

Figure 4–1
Ballpark view of the process architecture

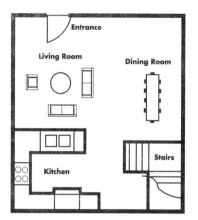

Figure 4–2
Classification theory at work

scious understanding that the shower belongs to a classification bathroom and not the classification living room.

There are two simple steps to defining the ballpark view of the process architecture.

1. Brainstorm potential high-level classes of processes such as sales, marketing, and manufacturing. These are called enterprise business functions.
2. Provide succinct definitions for each function and then begin to look for redundancy. Eliminate as much redundancy as possible by either modifying the list of functions or changing their definitions.

4.1 How to Classify

Although we have discussed the importance of classification, we have not yet discussed how the classification expert makes decisions on group boundaries. Why did we come up with classifications of animals like dogs, horses, and cows? Why didn't we classify them into animal groups based on color? So, instead of classifying animals into dogs, horses, and cows, we could have classified animals into "whanimals," which includes white dogs, horses, and cows, and "blanimals," which includes black dogs, horses, and cows. If you wanted to talk about a cow, you would talk about the whanimals and blanimals that give milk. Why doesn't this make sense to us?

4.2 The Concept of Discontinuity

Classification, as mentioned before, is the separation of "like" things into groups. An important fundamental in the field of classification is the con-

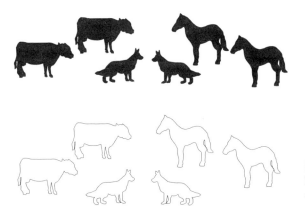

Figure 4–3
Deciding group boundaries in classification

cept of discontinuity—this concept helps you find the boundaries for groups of like things. Information engineering terms such as data affinity and state transitions also help find boundaries for groups of like things and are very similar concepts.

Criteria for classification differs depending on what you are classifying. Your criteria will obviously be different for classifying grades of potatoes than it would be for classifying grades of plutonium. For example, the classification of living things such as plants and animals relies on discontinuity between groups caused by natural selection. All plants and animals, we assume, came from the same primordial gak at some point, but natural selection based on a species' ability to survive has created larger and larger gaps between the species. These gaps between species are sometimes called the missing links. So, for the purposes of classifying living things, discontinuity is defined by the lack of intermediate forms between species. (There is no state transition in information technology terms.) For example, there are no known intermediate forms between a horse and a human; therefore they fall into distinct, discontinuous groups. Sometimes classes change. When a missing link is found, such as the apeman Australopithecus aferensis, it suggests that there was no gap of discontinuity, in this case between apes and humans. Perhaps early mythological creatures with, for example, the head of a snake and body of a lion may have been attempts to come to grips with these missing links (Figure 4–4).

It seems obvious to us now. We don't consider a snake to be in the same class as a lion. However, to get to this level of confidence in your classification scheme, you have to come to some conclusion as to your criteria for discontinuity.

Figure 4–4
Coming to grips with missing links between classes

Classification implies decision making. When you classify something, it means that you decide where it belongs. In biological classification terms, you have to decide if the ape is in the same class as a human or not. You can't sit on the fence if you are a classification expert. When classifying the colors, someone had to decide that red was an effect of light from 610 to 780 nanometers. Anything outside of that range was another color. Coming up with good classification criteria is not necessarily easy. I'm sure there was a lot of discussion and argument about color boundaries, especially if they had any of those racks of sample paint chips from the hardware store on hand.

Classification, in essence, sets standards. Just as in setting standards, classification decisions have to be made and they have to be made by people knowledgeable about the area being classified. Therefore business people have to classify information and processes in the enterprise. It cannot be delegated to information technology or administration any more than you would delegate the classification of fatal diseases to hospital administrators. Once confidence is gained around a classification scheme, people get pretty serious about it. "As a mycologist (a scientist who studies fungi) I enjoyed 'Stalking the Wild Mushroom,' but was surprised when the author referred to fungi as a plant. Fungi belong to a separate kingdom of taxonomy created solely for them, Kingdom Fungi. They are in no way related to plants."[1]

4.2.1 The Classification Concept of Discontinuity Applied to Information Architectures

It may seem odd to be discussing concepts such as fungi taxonomies and missing links when we are interested in things like order processing or inventory control. In reality there is a significant difference between

1. *Field and Stream*, September 1994: 8.

the more rigorous scientific approach to taxonomy and the less rigorous approach to classification. From Benjamin S. Bloom's famous *Taxonomy of Educational Objectives* comes a good definition of the difference:

> A classification scheme may be validated by reference to the criteria of communicability, usefulness, and suggestiveness; while a taxonomy must be validated by demonstrating its consistency with the theoretical views in research findings of the field it attempts to order. (p. 17)

Classification is useful because it improves the ability to communicate or, in other words, to process data. Just so we don't incur the wrath of the scientific community, we are really creating *classes* of processes and information in the enterprise, not *taxonomies* validated by carbon dating techniques.

We find discontinuity in the architecture by locating logical break points between groups of processes and data. These break points allow us to take a large, complex problem—the entire enterprise information architecture—and "chunk" it down into manageable pieces. These chunks can eventually be distributed or delegated for implementation while the architectural framework provides the central coordination. This is how we get the balance between central authority and distributed implementation that we talked about earlier. This is still much like having an architecture drawing that all the contractors have to follow but allowing each contractor to have enough freedom for efficient delivery of his or her piece of the construction effort.

It turns out that, for the purposes of designing the enterprise information architecture, our classification criteria are rather straightforward. Our classification criteria for data will be based around similarity in facts. The classification criteria for process will be based around similarity in activities. It is important to remember that classification criteria for data and process are significantly different. The original computer concept of **storing** data goes back to the idea of filing cabinets and is the equivalent of human memory. The concept of **processing** data comes from the idea of adding machines or calculators and provides the equivalent of human reasoning.[2]

You may have been hearing about the concept of "object orientation." Some people like to throw around new terms like OO, OODB, inheritance, and encapsulation just to impress you. Object orientation is

---

2. Theodore Roszak, *The Cult of Information*, 1986, p. 109.

basically classification theory, which, as you've heard earlier, is an ancient concept. Classification theory is not a technology, so hang in there because it is an important concept for business people to understand. We have some work to do in classifying the processes and information in our enterprise since they were not already done for us by Darwin, Plato, or Carl Linné. However, if we all work on this together, it is likely that we will come to some standard classes for each industry at some point. These standard classes will eventually allow us to integrate disparate applications, especially third party applications, more easily, leading to a true plug-and-play architecture within and between enterprises.

Classification theory abhors redundancy. As you work through your process and information classes and discover that something falls into more than one group, then classification theory requires you to resolve that redundancy. You can either change your classification scheme or create a new group and place that item in it to eliminate the redundancy. No Department of Redundancy Departments are allowed. Repeating groups and items are pulled out into separate groups. This is also an oversimplified explanation of Dr. Edgar F. Codd's relational database model, which he developed in 1969, and his concept of normal form for database design, developed shortly thereafter. Unfortunately, there are very few databases and even fewer architectures that truly utilize the concept of normal form to remove redundancy today.

We'll start slowly and use an easy example of process classification. Our fictitious enterprise is a small company. It is organized at the top level under two managers, a manufacturing manager and a marketing manager. We'll erroneously start by assuming that our organization chart makes a good process classification scheme. So we start with a manufacturing process class that contains all the activities that occur under the manufacturing manager and a marketing process class that contains all the activities that occur under the marketing manager. However, as we list all those activities, we already find redundancy—each department does its own hiring, so the hiring activity appears in both classes. Classification theory would insist that the hiring activity be separated out into a different functional class, apart from marketing and manufacturing. This removes the redundancy. Now the hiring activity appears in only one class. This does not mean that we need any organizational reporting changes; it just identifies that there is a separate hiring process class for the enterprise information architecture.

Enterprises have been unconsciously using classification theory to construct organization charts for many years. As the idea of mass production led to specialization of labor, companies had to classify like activities into areas of specialization to increase productivity and minimize redundancy. These classifications led to job or department definitions within the enterprise. If a function such as hiring existed in multiple places in an organization, sometimes it was pulled out and put in a separate organization as its own area of specialization—an organizational class so to speak. Let's assume that our company doesn't want to do that because it feels its manufacturing and marketing organizations are made more effective by having highly integrated personnel organizations. One of the most important points to understand when building an information architecture is that the way the company decides to organize has *nothing* to do with the information architecture.

We can still have the same manufacturing and marketing departments, but we have now three process classes in our enterprise information architecture: manufacturing, marketing, and hiring. We'll broaden the hiring class and call it "personnel." If you take that decision all the way down the Zachman framework to physical implementation of a system, you could choose to automate the personnel function once, not twice, and the software could be used by anyone who needed it, in this case by the manufacturing and marketing departments. Note that there isn't a personnel department in this example, but there is a personnel system. Unfortunately, think about how difficult it would be in today's vertical environment to build a system that was not sponsored by a particular department.

4.3 ORGANIZATIONAL CLASSIFICATION VERSUS PROCESS CLASSIFICATION

Remember that the criteria for classifying data and process are different. The criteria for classifying organizations of people are different also. It is very unlikely that the data classes and the process classes will map to your organizational structure in the enterprise. Human beings are not always organized around similar data or tasks for very good reasons.

Peter Drucker suggested quite a while ago that an effective organizational unit does not always have the same specialized activities.

> If we look at well-organized functional units, however, we shall find no such "bundle of skills." The typical sales department, for instance, includes selling activities, market research, pricing, market development, customer service, advertising and promotion, product development, often even responsibility for relationships with governmental

bodies and trade associations. But they work, indeed they work much better than units organized on similarity of skills—because they bring together all the specialized activities needed in one fairly sharply delimited stage of the work.[3]

In other words, effective organizations do not need to be classified by similar activities and in Drucker's opinion are more likely to be built around similar stages in a major process. Michael Hammer and James Champy, in the book *Reengineering the Corporation*, refined this concept. Reengineering encourages you to optimize the organization around major business processes such as order fulfillment or product generation which can be long strings of business activities that span many specialized departments today. A reengineering project might determine that you need to take previously specialized departments and distribute them back out to the major business processes. Rather than the enterprise being optimized around specialization, the reengineered enterprise is organizationally optimized for business process integration.

John Diebold had a very similar idea in 1952. "In discussing that specialized portion of the scientific revolution in industry called 'automation,' Diebold made the point that, in every instance, carrying it into practice encourages, when indeed it does not demand, the 'rethinking through' of each relevant process from beginning to end. This holds, as the automation reports testify, at once for the nature of the materials entering the plant, for all the machinery linked in successive steps in processing and manufacture, for the types of jobs and the training of the staff, for management control, for the types and uses of end products or services, and for most, if not all, of the routine office accounting and record keeping."[4] Diebold's "rethinking through" was the 1950 version of reengineering.

We sometimes like to blame the division of labor for disconnects in business processes. But we seem to be able to specialize along the production line and still make an end product that fits together. Both specialization (the division of labor) and business process integration are necessary in most enterprises just like on the assembly line, and we must learn how to make them both work.

This specialization and integration balance cannot be accomplished with the organization chart. Information and processes need to be inte-

---

3. *The Practice of Management*, 1956, p. 206.

4. Robert A. Brady, *Organization, Automation, and Society: The Scientific Revolution in Industry*, 1961, p. 13.

grated across the entire enterprise without expecting everyone in the enterprise to report directly to one manager. Organizations obviously must be departmentalized at some level just to manage span of control.

How a company decides to organize or reorganize should not impact the information architecture. Most companies choose one of the common organizational models, either by function, product, or location.[5] For example, the company may be organized around similar activities or processes like manufacturing or marketing. It may be organized around product lines or it may be organized around geographical location such as regional sales offices. Larger companies probably have a mix of these common organizational models.

Reengineering suggests a newer model—that is to organize around end-to-end business processes such as order fulfillment or product generation which likely span multiple functional departments in most enterprises. There are still other possible models such as organizing around customers.

4.4 BUSINESS PROCESS REENGINEERING VERSUS THE ENTERPRISE PROCESS ARCHITECTURE

It's important to understand that there has been a lot of discussion by experts on how to organize effectively. However, all organizational alternatives have disconnects somewhere except in the smallest of companies where everyone reports to one manager. Somehow, we have to figure out how to integrate the enterprise outside the boundaries of the organization chart. Even a company that reorganizes around reengineered business processes will not solve the entire integration problem.

For example, if you reorganize around a key business process such as order fulfillment, you may still have disconnects with other business processes such as product design. You will probably fall into the same trap of vertically aligning your systems with new organizations and finding new disconnects. That's why many reengineering projects keep expanding to encompass all the new disconnects until the project tries to swallow the whole enterprise in one gulp, leading to an extremely high failure rate. The information architecture holds the key to providing true enterprise integration and it must be decoupled from the organization chart, reengineered or not.

5. Fremont Kast and James Rosenzweig, *Organization and Management, A Systems Approach*, 1970, p. 180.

If you want to know how your organization is classified today, look at the organization charts. Remember that the business views of the enterprise information architecture are the foundation and must stand the test of time. Look again at the organization charts and see what date they were printed. Designing the boundaries of information systems around the organization chart is the main contributor to architectural instability. The foundation of the architecture must be buffered from organizational change. Therefore process classification for the architecture must not be based on the organizational classification scheme.

One of the original reasons for the vertical approach was to provide closer system alignment to the business problem at hand. But in many cases this vertical approach to systems development caused the business problems in the first place. If you base your system architecture around an organization chart, what do you do when the chart needs to change to take rapid advantage of a new business opportunity? Now you have a newly formed department with one or two incompatible departmental systems built around the obsolete organization chart. Since systems can't be replaced very quickly, most legacy systems today are still peaked to an organization structure of the past, reducing the ability to take full advantage of the new organization structure. Business process reengineering changes the organization chart, but not forever. The decoupling of data classification from process classification from organization classification allows freedom of movement in the enterprise. In an architected information environment, systems will no longer negatively impact organizational reporting changes and vice versa.

This is not to say that the constant change in organizational structure is bad. The organizational structure in a company needs to be extremely flexible so it is able to react quickly to take advantage of new market opportunities, newly acquired skills, or even a specific individual with unusual talents. By separating the enterprise information architecture into its data component, which is classified around facts, and its process component, which is classified around activities, the organization structure is freed to be classified around the human aspect of the enterprise. This is an important point to emphasize. The classification criteria for data, process, and organization are different.

For the purposes of the top two levels of the process architecture, the focus is on *what* is being done in the enterprise, not how it's done. As you move down the architecture, you will eventually need to define exactly *how* something needs to be done so that you can purchase or create software to automate it. It should be assumed that the enterprise will continually refine and improve *how* things are done for ongoing process improvement. This is again why the lower levels of the architecture are unstable.

Business process reengineering not only optimizes the organization around key business processes; it also provides an excellent methodology to improve how things are done within the process. But watch out! The *how* is very important when designing or purchasing an application in the lower levels of the architecture. You certainly have to know how you want to do something before you select a third party or develop an application. But some companies are defining the upper levels of the enterprise information architecture around the "how" work being done by the business process reengineering teams. It would be a mistake to assume that enterprises will reengineer their business processes only once. In fact, the term itself implies that it will be done again. Because of this, it is important not to define the strategic business views of the enterprise information architecture based on a single process reengineering effort. Obviously the "what" comes before the "how." The lower levels of the overall Zachman framework will deal with process or technology changes necessary to support the "how" of a reengineering effort. If the higher levels are done correctly, the lower levels will be able to change rapidly to accommodate the reengineered or re-reengineered processes over time.

Business process reengineering projects are usually appropriately limited to a subset of the enterprise for scope control. An effective enterprise information architecture can be built only if the whole of the enterprise is considered since valid classification schemes rely on a broad view of the area being classified. Can you imagine getting an architectural drawing for only half of a new high-rise? The business views of the enterprise information architecture should be completed prior to scoping any significant system project emerging out of a reengineering effort. Luckily, it should not take a lot of time. The enterprise information architecture is also very supportive of the business process reengineering effort. It will point out additional business breakthroughs that could assist reengineering efforts since it ferrets out redundancy driven by traditional views of the enterprise. It is likely that significant reengineering projects that need supporting information systems will not be successful without the framework provided by the enterprise information architecture.

4.5 THE BALLPARK VIEW OF ENTERPRISE BUSINESS PROCESSES

4.5.1 Step One: Brainstorming the Enterprise Business Functions

Step one of the ballpark view of the process architecture begins by brainstorming potential high-level classes of processes. We'll call these enterprise business functions. These functions are the highest-level groupings of like activities in the enterprise. Remember, we're just sketching the process architecture at this point. Each industry obviously has different functions. For the sake of developing an example, we'll use the discrete manufacturing industry. Within an industry like discrete manufacturing, there are probably some fairly typical enterprise business functions such as those shown in Figure 4–5.

R&D

Production

Marketing

Sales

Distribution

Service

Finance & Accounting

Personnel

Figure 4–5
Typical discrete manufacturing business functions

Discrete manufacturing companies may have different names for some of these functions, but their basic descriptions will most likely be similar to the following:

R&D	Designs the products and services of the enterprise
Production	Produces the products and services of the enterprise
Marketing	Generates demand for the enterprise products and services
Sales	Obtains agreements from customers to purchase products and services

Distribution	Delivers the products of the enterprise to the marketplace
Service	Delivers services other than products or goods
Finance and accounting	Manages the assets of the enterprise
Personnel	Hires, develops, and manages human resources necessary to support the production and delivery of the products and services

Remember that we are not defining an organization chart here. You may have combined parts of these functions into organizations to optimize a cross-functional business process such as order fulfillment.

4.5.2 Step Two: Define the Functions and Look for Redundancy

Even at this high level of business function definition, we do not yet have the functions classified cleanly in the list above. As an example, one of the definitions raises a classification question. If we define distribution as the delivery of goods only to the marketplace, the production function encompasses a similar distribution function when semifinished goods are distributed to another final assembly plant during the production process. We now have a classification problem to resolve because the basic distribution function appears in two places. It is hard to look at shipping something to a final assembly plant as a discontinuous process from shipping something to a customer. Don't you think Plato would put those two things in the same process class? Therefore the function of distribution as defined is not yet discontinuous with production in the above classification scheme. In this case, we don't need to create a new class. If we broaden the definition of distribution function to allow for the delivery of products to an organization that is either internal or external, it would include the internal distribution that used to be part of the manufacturing class and makes it a discontinuous class from everything else. The redundancy goes away. Remember, this does not mean that you need to form a distribution organization that handles all distribution functions. We are defining the information architecture, not the organization chart.

Another problem comes to mind. Procurement or purchasing activities happen in many of the currently listed functions. For example, production purchases materials and perhaps marketing purchases literature. This would be a good example of a function that may need to be pulled out and made its own function to reduce redundancy.

So we'll create a draft of our ballpark view of the process architecture by broadening our definition of the distribution function and adding a procurement function.

Ballpark View Process Classes

R&D	Designs the products and services of the enterprise
Production	Produces the products and services of the enterprise
Marketing	Generates demand for the enterprise products and services
Sales	Obtains agreements from customers to purchase products and services
Distribution	Delivers the products and services of the enterprise to a location
Service	Delivers the services of the enterprise other than products or goods
Procurement	Obtains products and services for the enterprise
Finance and accounting	Manages the assets of the enterprise
Personnel	Hires, develops, and manages human resources necessary to support the production and delivery of the products and services

It's important not to get hung up on perfection in the ballpark view. When you exit the ballpark view of the process architecture, a comfortable set of five to ten business functions is a good start.

Defining the ballpark view of the process architecture is usually pretty easy, although it sometimes generates some good business discussion. At this point, we are ready to move on to the ballpark view of the data architecture.

The Ballpark View of the Data Architecture

We now move from the ballpark view of processes to the ballpark view of data. The word "data" sounds technical and sometimes scares business people away. **The business views of the data architecture are critical to your success.** This is where you solve the information problems in your enterprise. The unique value that the data architecture provides is form over function. Data is form; process is function.

The data architecture is designed around the ten to twenty company assets that are critically important for the enterprise to meet its

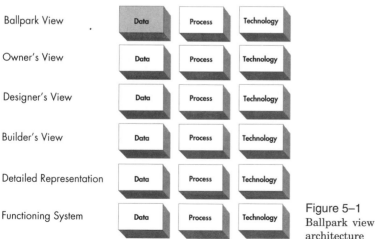

Ballpark View	Data	Process	Technology
Owner's View	Data	Process	Technology
Designer's View	Data	Process	Technology
Builder's View	Data	Process	Technology
Detailed Representation	Data	Process	Technology
Functioning System	Data	Process	Technology

Figure 5–1
Ballpark view of the data architecture

77

mission, assets like customers, material, and money. The data architecture is more critical than the process architecture because most business processes exist to manage the assets, not the other way around. If you have a good understanding of the assets you are managing defined by the data architecture, the processes tend to define themselves. Most information systems developers take a completely opposite and *wrong* approach. Most designers focus on the processes that need automating, not on which asset is being managed. A process-centric approach will *always* create a fragmented, redundant architecture. A data-centric approach creates a highly integrated, streamlined architecture. In fact, a data-centric approach will reengineer processes as a by-product.

The fact that the data architecture is anchored around key assets of the company provides stability to the architecture. For this reason, the data architecture is the foundation to the rest of the architecture. James Martin, a well-known expert in the area of information engineering, emphasizes these points. "The basic premise of information engineering is that data lie at the center of modern data processing....A second basic premise of information engineering is that the types of data used in an enterprise do not change very much."[1] These two premises drive a competent architect to focus on data more than process.

There are three steps to building the ballpark view of the data architecture.

1. Brainstorm potential data classes for each enterprise business function defined earlier in the ballpark process architecture.
2. Look for similarities and generalize the potential data classes into first-pass global data classes.
3. Use data modeling techniques to refine the global data classes.

When we've completed steps one and two, we will have a draft of a set of global data classes that represents all of our originally brainstormed data classes. Step three will test these global data classes and refine them. But before we undertake these steps, we will need to learn a new technique called "data modeling."

5.1 DATA MODELING

When we are classifying data in the business views of the architecture, we are actually performing a high-level data modeling exercise. Data

---

1. *Information Engineering, Book I,* 1989, p. 57.

models in the business views of the architecture are **business** models, not technical models. Time to take a bus ride.

Data models were introduced in the last few decades as an excellent way to understand the information needs of an enterprise. Most of the original work on data modeling was done in the 1970s by people like Peter Chen and Dr. E. F. Codd. In the late 1970s, the concept of information engineering with its diagramming techniques for process and data was jointly developed by Clive Finkelstein and James Martin. Martin's diagramming techniques appear in many computer-aided software engineering (CASE) tools.

Also during the late 1970s, Robert Brown, a consultant at Lockheed, created a data modeling technique that he eventually utilized at the Bank of America. At the bank, it was called ADAM. At about the same time, the U.S. Air Force, as part of its integrated computer-aided manufacturing (ICAM) efforts, identified three diagramming techniques for defining process and data models. They were called IDEF methods which was short for ICAM DEFinition. IDEF0 was the function modeling technique; IDEF1 was the data method that was jointly developed by Hughes Aircraft and the D. Appleton Company (DACOM); IDEF2 was the dynamics or behavior modeling technique. In 1985, the concepts of ADAM replaced IDEF1 and its name was changed to IDEF1X with the X standing for extended. As an air force standard, IDEF1X is now in the public domain. Unfortunately, not a lot of documentation is available on it, so most people utilize the Chen or Martin conventions for data modeling. However, in the future, IDEF1X may become the standard because it is part of the public domain.[2]

Data models provide a way of describing data of interest to a company. Data models can be created for all levels of abstraction from the business views down to the physical data models that become the actual database schema running on a computer. Data modeling is an exercise in classification. In the ballpark view, we are only interested in determining high-level classes of data. Classes of data are called "entities" in data modeling terminology. Examples of entities are customers, products, or orders. A data model also describes relationships between entities. For example, customers place orders (hopefully).

The data model becomes more precise and detailed as it moves down the levels of abstraction provided by the Zachman framework. Glo-

2. Thomas A. Bruce, *Designing Quality Databases with IDEF1X Information Models*, 1992, p. xii.

bal data classes are the highest level of abstraction of the data architecture. They are groups of data classes or entities which will become multiple entities lower in the architecture which eventually become physical tables in a database. The same diagramming techniques apply when modeling entities at any level of the architecture. The main purpose of data modeling in the business views of the architecture is to help us validate that we have classified the data architecture correctly, not to design a database. Therefore, our data models will not be as complex as the data models that some of us have seen wallpapered on the side of a database designer's cubicle.

In order to participate more fully in designing the business views of the architecture, everyone will need to be knowledgeable about data modeling concepts.

5.1.1 Relationships versus Entities

Data modeling is much like sentence diagramming. Find the subject of the sentence and you'll find an entity or data class. When you are modeling, you may hear someone define a potential entity as an "X that does Y." The next person defines another potential entity as an "X that does Z." Separate out the subject X and you will find a true entity. If there is an object to the sentence, the verbs define a relationship to another potential entity. For example, we first define a potential entity *cart horse* as **a horse that pulls a cart** and another potential entity *racehorse* as **a horse that runs a race**. You have probably discovered the true entities *horse, race,* and *cart.*

It's that simple. Subject, predicate, object—terms we probably haven't heard since elementary school. Interestingly enough, predicate logic or functional calculus is a fundamental in information processing. Remember $f(x)$? F is function or process and x is the variable or data.

It may surprise you that the Reverend Charles Lutwidge Dodgson, otherwise known as Lewis Carroll, not only wrote *Alice in Wonderland* but also wrote one of the most brilliant textbooks on symbolic logic, another related information processing field. His important work was in three parts. Part I begins: "The universe contains Things. (For example, 'I', 'London', 'roses',).... Things have attributes. (For example, 'large', 'red', 'old'.)"[3] Things and attributes, as Dr. Dodgson described back in the 1800s, are fundamental data modeling concepts.

---

3. *Symbolic Logic*, ed. William Warren Bartley III, 1977, p. 59.

In a data model, nouns likely are entities and verbs are relationships. Most data classes or entities have relationships to other entities. The horse pulls the cart. The horse and the cart are two separate things, but they have a relationship—the verb "pull." It is important to separate a relationship from entities in the ballpark view of the enterprise information architecture because that is usually how redundancy can be eliminated. Many times, these relationships represent different organizational views of the same thing. A cart horse and racehorse are transformed to be a horse that pulls a cart and a horse that runs a race. Note that the concepts of racehorse and cart horse go away and are replaced by the concepts of a horse, race, and cart with the relationships run and pull.

Getting the data classes or entities right is a critical concept to defining the enterprise information architecture because it removes redundancy and simplifies the architecture. In the horse example above, the data that is collected and stored about the horse itself would be stored only once in an architected environment. In an unarchitected environment, the horse's size, color, weight, and so on would be stored twice if the same horse was both a cart horse and a racehorse, three times if it was also a show horse.

Redundancy is probably the biggest problem in today's current information systems. The same "thing" shows up in a myriad of vertical, process-centric databases in most companies—for example, prospect, customer, supplier, freight forwarder. These are all closely related things. They are all organizations that we have a business relationship with. Correctly classifying the data architecture integrates information across the enterprise. If you don't get the data classes right, the data architecture *dis*integrates the enterprise.

5.1.2 Diagramming Techniques for Data Modeling

An entity relationship diagram (ERD) is the tool used to illustrate data classes (entities) and their relationships with each other. It is a relatively simple technique to understand, and, in the business views of the architecture, it is a *business* diagram, not a technical diagram. An ERD helps separate entities from relationships while still capturing the importance of the relationship.

In an ERD, data classes or entities are shown as boxes. Relationships are shown as lines. That's not so hard is it? There are various entity-relationship diagramming techniques that can be used. Although

IDEF1X may eventually be the standard, it is not heavily utilized today. For the sake of simplicity, we'll choose James Martin's convention and demonstrate using the horse, cart, and race example. We have three entities and two relationships. Therefore, we draw three boxes and two lines (see Figure 5–2).

Now we add to the diagram some notation to describe the numerical component of the relationship. (Data modelers call this notation "cardinality" and "optionality," but you don't need to worry about those terms.) The numerical component of the relationship is specified at both ends of the relationship line between entities. We will define the minimum and maximum of each relationship, choosing either zero or one as the minimum (optionality) and one or many as the maximum (cardinality). For example, let's define the minimum relationship between the entities. Does every horse have to pull a cart? No, we can have pasture potatoes that just sit around and eat hay. So the lowest possible number of relationships between a horse and a cart is zero. The relationship is optional. The same goes for a horse and a race since not all horses run races. Now we need to ask what the maximum relationships are between these entities. A horse could potentially pull many carts and run many races in its lifetime. Therefore, the maximum relationship is many in both cases. We now know what the minimum and maximum relationships are between the entity horse and the other two entities. We indicate that on the diagram by putting a zero on the relationship line along with a notation that looks like an upside down "v" to represent many (Figure 5–3).

This diagram reads, "A horse can pull zero or many carts and run zero or many races." Now we have to do it for the other end of the rela-

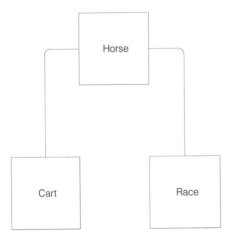

Figure 5–2

All data models throughout this book have been prepared using EasyCASE Professional v4.2, a product from Evergreen Software Tools, Inc., of Redmond, Washington. Used with permission.

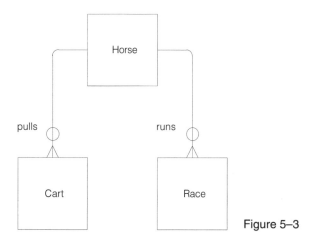

Figure 5–3

tionships. Does a cart ever have to be pulled by a horse? Nope. It can also sit around in a museum. But some carts are pulled by many horses. Therefore, the numerical component of the relationship from cart to horse is zero or many. A cart can be pulled by zero or many horses. Now let's look at the relationship between race and horse. Can a race be run with zero horses? No; therefore the minimum is at least one. It is not an optional relationship. What's the maximum number of horses in a race? Again, it is many. Therefore the relationship between race and horse is one or many. A race can be run by one or many horses. Figure 5–4 shows what the final ERD looks like.

The finished diagram is read, "A horse pulls zero or many carts and runs zero or many races. A cart can be pulled by zero or many horses, and

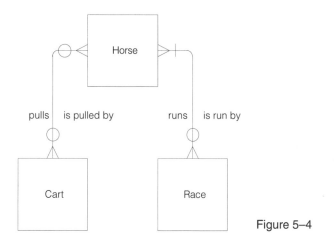

Figure 5–4

a race is run by one or many horses." That covers the basic data modeling terminology and diagramming conventions.

5.1.3 Recursive Relationships

There are a few more difficult concepts to understand in the area of entity relationships. Some entities (data classes) can have a relationship with themselves. Sounds kind of lonely, doesn't it? As an example, if you ran a private school, you would probably define an important entity called *student*. The information you want to know about a student is perhaps the identity of his or her parents and their billing address. With this high-level model of students, further down in the Zachman framework you would have a database record for each student that included the parents' names and billing address. Now the second child from that family enrolls. Uh-oh—creeping redundancy. Now the parent and address data appear in both students' records. We have a classification scheme problem.

A second entity, you cry! So now we have entities *students* and *parents* with a relationship between them. So that we don't have to get into biological parents versus stepparents and adoptive parents, we'll just assume a student can have many parents and a parent can have many students. We'll also assume that a student has at least one person he or she can call a parent and that a parent has at least one student in this school; otherwise we wouldn't be worried about them at all in our business model. Figure 5–5 shows our improved model.

Not so fast—we're still not done. You now find out that the student is pregnant and will be enrolling her newborn in the school's infant care program. So now the student is also a parent. Something is still wrong with our classification scheme.

The parent/student example can be resolved with what is called a recursive relationship. Even though recursive or involuted relationships are some of the more difficult relationship concepts to understand, they happen quite often in industry. A bill of material is a recursive relationship. It describes that a product can be a part of another product. An organization chart is a recursive relationship. An

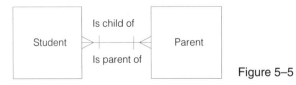

Figure 5–5

organization reports to another organization and so on up the chain. Recursive relationships can remove significant redundancy, so they are important to watch for.

In our private school example, an entity should have emerged called *person*. Plato and Darwin would have found it. Obviously there is a lot of similarity in the broad sense of the universe between a parent, student, and child. They are all humans. You don't have to call the entity *Homo sapiens* in your enterprise ERD, but something like *person* or *individual* would work. This particular entity is related to itself in many ways. Mother, father, sister, brother, daughter, son, wife, husband, student, teacher, employee, manager—all of these are relationships between humans, not different things. Thank goodness you don't need to know about all the relationships between people in most enterprises, but you do need to separate relationships between people from the people themselves. For example, a manager is a *person* who has another person working for him or her. In our school example, the parents we are concerned with are parents of at least one person in the school. The person enrolled can be a child of one or many parents. When drawing the ERD, we show the recursive relationship by drawing a line from the entity back to itself (Figure 5–6).

5.1.4 Roles

Another more difficult relationship to understand is a role relationship. Previously, we worked to separate relationships from entities. However, it turns out that some relationships turn into entities. Sometimes the relationship itself is so critical that you want to keep a great deal of data about it. If a person buys many times from you or you anticipate that he or she will, you would like to retain information about that relationship to use over and over again—for example, a customer number or buying preferences. These types of relationships are called "roles." Roles are entities holding information about relationships.

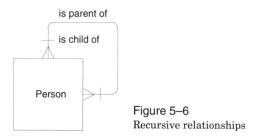

Figure 5–6
Recursive relationships

In our school example, although we now can tell who is the parent of the child, we still want to store information about the role of student that only a subset of our entity *persons* plays. So we add an entity *students* and attach it to the entity *persons* as shown in Figure 5–7.

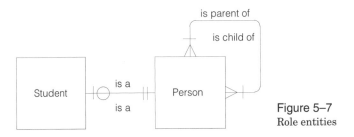

Figure 5–7
Role entities

This ERD reads that a student is one and only one person and a person can be zero or one student indicating that not all of our persons are students. Further down the Zachman framework, the student database record would hold information related to the person's role as a student such as a student number. The *person* database record would hold generic attributes about people such as their names and ages.

As a business example of a relationship that might turn into a role and therefore an entity, let's talk about customers and vendors. We might start by assuming those are two different entities—*vendor* and *customer*. We go through the relationship-versus-entity discussion and conclude that there is a new entity or class called *person* that we know is either a customer or vendor or both by its relationship to a sales order and/or an internal purchase order.

The diagram in Figure 5–8 reads, "A person can accept zero or many

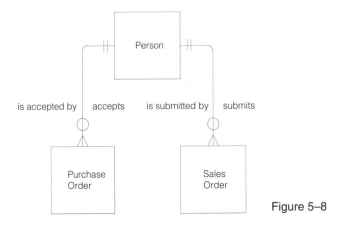

Figure 5–8

of our purchase orders, and a person can submit zero or many sales orders." We could just assume that, if a person accepts at least one of our purchase orders, he or she is a vendor; if a person places at least one sales order, he or she is a customer. But if we wanted to store some data about that organization's relationship with us as a customer or vendor, we don't have a class to put it in. We could put it in the *person* class, but data about a customer role is pertinent only if there is a required relationship between person and sales order. And the same is true with data about a vendor role.

The fact that we want to store data about the relationship tells us to create role entities, as in Figure 5–9. In this example, people can play a role called "customer" who can place a sales order. People can also play a role called "vendor" who can supply against our purchase order.

In this particular case, we've returned to our original proposed entities of *customer* and *vendor*, but we've gained insight by understanding that there is a new entity called *person* that reduces redundancy and integrates the enterprise view of our business partners.

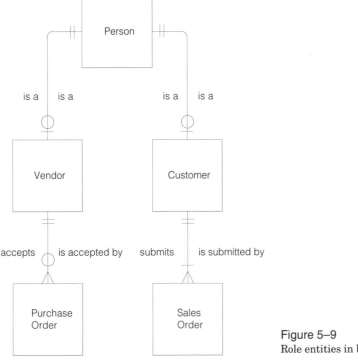

Figure 5–9
Role entities in business

5.1.5 Resource Life Cycles or State Transitions

The resources of an enterprise go through a life cycle. Typically, there is a planning cycle for the resource, followed by obtaining the resource, followed by managing the resource, followed by disposal or retirement. For example, employees go through a life cycle from human resource planning, hiring, managing, and termination. One classification trap to avoid is putting things in different parts of their life cycles into separate classes. For example, a customer's purchase order and the internal view of that purchase order, usually called a sales order, are really the same thing in two different states, submitted and received. Just because we take a customer's purchase order and enter it into our own order processing system doesn't make it a different thing. It is interesting to note that we even give the customer's purchase order our own number almost as if to prove to ourselves that it isn't the same thing. In an architected environment, we would consider these the same thing in different parts of its life cycle, as in Figure 5–10.

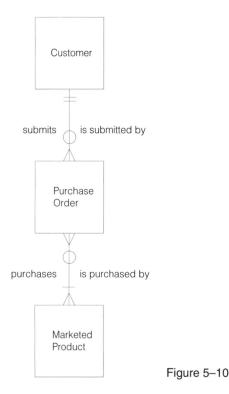

Figure 5–10

The ERD in Figure 5–9 is read, " A customer submits zero or many purchase orders. A purchase order is submitted from one and only one customer. A purchase order has one or many marketed products, and a marketed product can be on zero or many purchase orders."

5.2 STEP ONE: BRAINSTORM POTENTIAL DATA CLASSES

At the ballpark level of the data architecture, we are concerned with high-level grouping of things important to the enterprise and their inter-relationships. In step one, we brainstorm a list of potential data classes or entities important to each of the enterprise business functions identified in the ballpark view of the process architecture. There are many examples of potential data classes available as a starting point from various data modeling or information engineering books. For a manufacturing company, a brainstormed list might look like Figure 5–11.

You will most likely brainstorm about two to ten potential data classes or entities per enterprise business function depending on what level of abstraction you are comfortable with. Remember, perfection is not the goal in the ballpark view since we will have the opportunity to refine and iterate this list in the next steps of the ballpark view and during the development of the business owner's view.

Function/Data

R&D	Sales
Products	Territories
Procurement	Sales Reps
Materials	Sales Offices
Vendors	Quotas
Internal Purchase Orders	Forecasts
Production	Sales Deals
WIP	Customers
Facilities	Customer Purchase Orders
Marketing	Distribution
Markets	Sales Orders
Prospects	FGI
Leads	Warehouses
Prices	Shipments
Service	Invoices
Services	F&A
Service Contracts	Costs
Service Deliveries	Revenues
Parts	Budgets
	Personnel
	Employees
	Compensation

Figure 5–11
Potential data classes

5.3 STEP TWO: GENERALIZE INTO GLOBAL DATA CLASSES

When classifying information, much like classifying anything, we want to look for similarities. This requires that we remove the organizational views of data. Like Plato, we are searching here for facts, not opinions. Insist on definitions. Ask the question, "What is it?" Don't worry about what it does for now.

When attempting to classify, it is appropriate to bounce between generalization and specification as a useful tool for debate. In addition, it is helpful to use the Greeks' bias toward seeing things in their larger context. That is why we start with generalization. Lean toward lumping even slightly related things together and then try to prove discontinuity versus assuming things are different right up front. In other words, put the horses and zebras together first before you assume they are different things. By putting them together first, you will more easily see the similarities. You should encourage more arguments about how things are the same than how they are different. This will ensure a bias toward simplicity. Our western culture of individualism makes us all nitpickers by nature and adds complexity to our lives and our workplace.

Let's take the potential list of data classes and see if we can find some natural groupings to form a more generalized list of global data classes. Sometimes reverting to childlike simplicity works best. Is it a person, place, or thing? For the purposes of running an enterprise, we'll add events or transactions (see Figure 5–12).

Person	Place	Thing	Event
Vendors	Facilities	Products	Leads
Customers	Sales Offices	Prices	Sales Deals
Sales Reps	Warehouses	Services	Purchase Orders
Employees		Materials	Customer Purchase Orders
Prospects		WIP	Sales Orders
Markets		FGI	Shipments
Territories		Parts	Invoices
			Service Contracts
			Service Deliveries
			Budgets
			Forecasts
			Quotas
			Revenues
			Costs
			Compensation

Figure 5–12
Draft set of global data classes

5.4 STEP THREE: USE DATA MODELING TECHNIQUES TO REFINE THE GLOBAL DATA CLASSES

Hopefully, even the novice architect can begin to see the magnitude of potential redundancy of data. At this point, we will take each draft global data class, look for discontinuity between its data classes or entities, and refine our global data classes.

5.4.1 Global Data Class Person

You can see that our original list of entities within the global data class Person includes some roles such as *vendors, customers, sales reps, employees,* and *prospects*. If we utilize the data model that we came up with earlier, we need to introduce the entity *people* that can play one or many of those roles. That way, the basic information about the person (or the organization the person reports to) is only stored once with the information about the roles the person plays stored in the role entities.

So let's make our first change in our potential entity list. We'll add an entity *people* in the global data class Person. As an aside, in many companies that sell business to business as opposed to business to consumer, customers are considered to be organizations, not people. This is a pragmatic approach to physical system design if you can't afford to collect information about the people involved in either the purchase or the sale. However, in the business view of the architecture it is probably a mistake to think that companies buy from you, not people. Companies are just groups of people. Someone, somewhere, is signing that purchase order. With the shift from mass marketing to direct marketing, it will be increasingly important to understand the needs of individuals regardless of whether they are part of a large company or not. However, organizations are also something we probably need to know about, so we'll add that as an entity also.

Now, are all the rest of the entities under the current global data class Person continuous? It doesn't seem like the role entities are all directly related to each other. By creating the new entities *people* and *organizations*, we have removed the commonality or redundancy that existed within all the rest of the role entities. Although there doesn't seem to be anything in common with all the role entities, some of them have some commonality with each other. First, the role of *sales reps* can be played by an *employee*, so we'll group those two together for now. Since *vendors* don't seem related to any other role or state, we'll keep it separate.

We now have the remaining role entities *customers, prospects, markets*, and *territories* in Figure 5–13. Are they discontinuous? Let's think about what a market or territory is. Isn't it really just a group of potential customers or prospects? Even though you may call a market or territory something like "manufacturing companies west of I405," at some point, you will know the list of prospects or customers that are included, won't you? If we look at markets and territories like this, they can be considered the planning state of prospects and customers. If we take that viewpoint, the group is continuous and can be left alone. We now have four logical groupings of entities replacing the more generalized global data class of Person.

Person	Place	Thing	Event
People	Facilities	Products	Leads
Organizations	Sales Offices	Prices	Sales Deals
	Warehouses	Services	Purchase Orders
		Materials	Customer Purchase Orders
Vendors		WIP	Sales Orders
		FGI	Shipments
Sales Reps		Parts	Invoices
Employees			Service Contracts
			Service Deliveries
Customers			Budgets
Prospects			Forecasts
Markets			Quotas
Territories			Revenues
			Costs
			Compensation

Figure 5–13

5.4.2 Global Data Class Place

The original entities under the global data class Place were roles that a place can play such as *facility, warehouse,* and *sales office*. We need to introduce an entity *places* (or potentially *buildings*) and again separate it from its roles, which removes most of the commonality or redundancy of data found in the original role entities. Since there doesn't seem to be any commonality between the role entities, we'll let them be their own classes. That gives us four new global data classes that replace the original global data class Place (Figure 5–14).

5.4.3 Global Data Class Thing

Products and parts are sometimes viewed as discontinuous groups with products defined as the finished good that is sold and parts defined

Person	Place	Thing	Event
People	Places	Products	Leads
Organizations		Prices	Sales Deals
	Facilities	Services	Purchase Orders
		Materials	Customer Purchase Orders
Vendors	Sales Offices	WIP	Sales Orders
		FGI	Shipments
Sales Reps	Warehouses	Parts	Invoices
Employees			Service Contracts
			Service Deliveries
Customers			Budgets
Prospects			Forecasts
Markets			Quotas
Territories			Revenues
			Costs
			Compensation

Figure 5–14

as the components that went into the product. However, this viewpoint seems to introduce a classification problem because in many companies parts can also be sold as products.

Just to get yourself out of the departmental view of products and parts, take yourself back to 500 B.C. You and your best friend Plato are having a philosophical argument. You say, "Let's assume there is an enterprise that is in the automobile industry." (Plato isn't sure what you're talking about but he's still listening.) "Division One manufactures and sell wheels directly to the public and also supplies them to Division Two who makes cars. Division One also manufactures engines for Division Two but does not sell them direct to the public. Division Two assembles and sells cars utilizing the wheels and engines supplied by Division One. Now, Division One believes the wheel belongs in the class called Products and the engine in the class called Parts. Division Two believes the wheel and the engine are in the class called Parts and the car is in the class called Products. Which is correct?"

Plato responds, "Let's put the wheel that was sold to the customer from Division One next to the wheel that was on the car that Division Two produced. They have the exact same physical properties. Is the wheel that Division One sells discontinuous from the wheel that Division Two puts on its cars? Of course not. Is the fact that the wheel can act as both a part and a product important? Of course. Those are roles that the wheel can play. So for now we'll redefine our data class called Products as 'something physical that is produced.'" (The dictionary is an excellent noncontroversial source for data class names and definitions.) We haven't said anything about whether a product is sold directly to a customer or used as a manufacturing component in our definition, so engines, wheels, and cars all belong to this information class at this point.

5.4.4 The Importance of Class Membership

The entire process of classification assumes that there can be no overlap between groups. If there is, the classification scheme is wrong. Therefore class membership must be precisely defined. A human is a member of the species Homo sapiens and no other. The basic characteristics of a wheel cannot belong to two different classes. However, a wheel can play the role of product or part or both.

5.4.5 Classification Difficulties

Classification can sometimes be difficult. For example, determining the criteria for class membership can be difficult If there is limited or incomplete knowledge about a particular area, (limited specimens in scientific terms), it is hard to come up with a stable classification scheme. With limited knowledge, the classification expert will tend to classify with too narrow a viewpoint. This is why scientists insist on many specimens before they classify a plant or animal. This is also the key reason why it is so important to examine the entire enterprise when designing the business views of the architecture.

For example, if you have no "specimens" in your enterprise that have a part used as both a manufacturing component and a marketed product, it will be hard to see the similarity. Succinct definitions of class membership greatly assist in situations like this. When you begin struggling with the definition of a part and a product because they both start with the words "a material that," you know you have a problem. Class definitions must not be ambiguous. For a lesson on ambiguity, we'll turn to FBI director J. Edgar Hoover. He didn't like the format of one of his letters, so he scrawled a note on the bottom—"watch the borders"—and gave it back to his assistant. Of course, the assistant immediately dispatched FBI agents to the Canadian and Mexican borders.[4] Class definitions need to be well understood by everyone.

Let's extend our earlier example of the automobile enterprise and look at some other classification problems. Talk to Plato again. Division Three of Enterprise A sells service on the cars of Division Two. The enterprise has a classification decision to make. Are products and the service

4. Roger Von Oech, *A Whack on the Side of the Head*, 1983, p. 76.

in the same class? Marketing views products and services as the same entity because they are both sold to customers. However, we just redefined the entity Products as something physical that is produced. Things like wheels, engines, and cars are in this data class. Is service similar enough to put in the same class? Service isn't really produced in the sense of manufacturing. It doesn't seem similar enough to merit keeping it in the same classification. (However, the parts that service uses to repair the car do seem to fit in the data class Products.)

Here is what would make Plato roll his eyes. In most enterprises, the wheel that is sold directly and the wheel that is part of a car would seem discontinuous because of our departmental separation between manufacturing and marketing. In those same enterprises, products and services would probably be considered a continuous group. If you had two wheels and a person all in a row, which would you put together? There are kindergarten handouts that answer that question for you.

Same or Different?

Circle the thing that is different

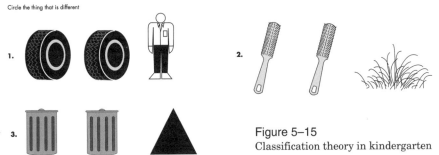

Figure 5–15
Classification theory in kindergarten

Remember "animal, mineral, vegetable?" Wheels and humans should not be put in the same class.

However, the **role** of being marketed is shared by both physical products and services. For instance, they would both have some kind of price. So we need to introduce a new entity we'll call *market offerings* to cover the role of being sold. Both products and services can be sold as a market offering. Much like products being redefined to be a physical thing, services becomes redefined around the concept of labor. The entity *services* is now also much more generic. This kind of accurate modeling increases flexibility in the architecture. For example, now service can share the role of market offering with products, even if you don't intend to provide that kind of market offering today. An ERD for this whole area could look something like Figure 5–16.

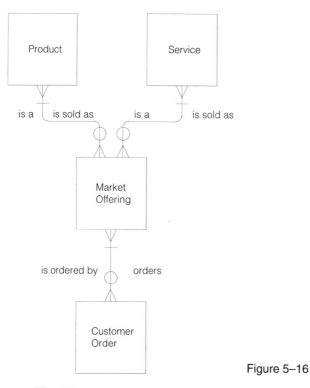

Figure 5–16

The ERD shown in this figure indicates that products (things) and services (labor-oriented deliveries) can be sold as a market offering on a customer order but don't ever have to be sold. This model also opens our eyes to the possibility that many products and services could be included in a single market offering.

Role entities have a very interesting ability to tell you about previously unseen competitive situations or growth areas. As an example, if you did discover that market offering is just a role that a product or service can play, perhaps you haven't seen the possibility of selling some of your other internal products or services that don't currently play the role of a *market offering*.

We have transformed our earlier concept of product to be things that are physically produced such as material, parts, work in progress (WIP), and finished goods inventory (FGI). Therefore, when a product is both included in an intermediate assembly and sold directly to customers, the redundant information stored about the product is eliminated. The basic attributes of the product such as size, weight, description, and cost are stored only once regardless of whether it is a product that is sold or a product that is used as a part in the internal manufacturing processes. The entities of *parts* and *market offerings* can now be considered roles that a product or physical thing can play. For example, in the role entity of *part*, you may want to keep information like dimensions or heat sensitivity. In the role entity of *market offering*, you will want to store price. Relationships can be tied to specific roles too. For example, a relationship to sales channel is appropriate only to a product or service's role as a market offering.

Let's indicate some of our new groupings based on roles under the global data class Thing. We redefined Products to be something physical that is produced. That view of product is tightly related to the entities, *materials*, *WIP*, *FGI*, and *parts,* so we'll group those together. These physical things are not related to *services*, so we'll leave *services* in its own group for now. Since the role of *market offerings* can be played by both products and services, classification theory says it must be pulled out into its own group. The entity type *prices* belongs with this group. That gives us three refined global data classes to replace the original global data class Thing in Figure 5–17.

Person	Place	Thing	Event
People	Places	Products	Leads
Organizations		Materials	Sales Deals
	Facilities	WIP	Purchase Orders
		FGI	Customer Purchase Orders
Vendors	Sales Offices	Parts	Sales Orders
			Shipments
Sales Reps	Warehouses	Services	Invoices
Employees			Service Contracts
		Market Offerings	Service Deliveries
Customers		Prices	Budgets
Prospects			Forecasts
Markets			Quotas
Territories			Revenues
			Costs
			Compensation

Figure 5–17

5.4.6 Global Data Class Event

Not all the events have something in common. However, it seems there are several likely groups of events that do have something in common. For example, *leads* and *sales deals* are initial stages of a customer need, a need that sometimes continues on to *customer purchase order, sales order, shipment*, and *invoice*. We'll group those entities together for now in Figure 5–18. Note that the actual payment of the invoice or what we have called "revenue" may not be continuous with the customer need life cycle. In classification terms, invoice and revenue are discontinuous. In data modeling terms, there is no state transition.

Person	Place	Thing	Event
People	Places	Products	Leads
Organizations		Materials	Sales Deals
	Facilities	WIP	Customer Purchase Orders
		FGI	Sales Orders
Vendors	Sales Offices	Parts	Shipments
			Invoices
Sales Reps	Warehouses	Services	
Employees			Purchase Orders
		Market Offerings	Service Contracts
Customers		Prices	Service Deliveries
Prospects			Budgets
Markets			Forecasts
Territories			Quotas
			Revenues
			Costs
			Compensation

Figure 5–18

Continuing on down the list of Event entities, *purchase orders* are internal orders from vendors typically for material. Therefore, we'll group *purchase orders* with the role of *vendors* in Figure 5–19.

Person	Place	Thing	Event
People	Places	Products	Leads
Organizations		Materials	Sales Deals
	Facilities	WIP	Customer Purchase Orders
		FGI	Sales Orders
Vendors	Sales Offices	Parts	Shipments
Purchase Orders			Invoices
	Warehouses	Services	
Sales Reps			Service Contracts
Employees		Market Offerings	Service Deliveries
		Prices	Budgets
Customers			Forecasts
Prospects			Quotas
Markets			Revenues
Territories			Costs
			Compensation

Figure 5–19

Service contracts and *service deliveries* are much like the idea of *customer orders* and *shipments* but, because they are people oriented versus thing oriented, we'll put them in a separate class in Figure 5–20.

Person	Place	Thing	Event
People	Places	Products	Leads
Organizations		Materials	Sales Deals
	Facilities	WIP	Customer Purchase Orders
		FGI	Sales Orders
Vendors	Sales Offices	Parts	Shipments
Purchase Orders			Invoices
	Warehouses	Services	
Sales Reps			Service Contracts
Employees		Market Offerings	Service Deliveries
		Prices	
Customers			Budgets
Prospects			Forecasts
Markets			Quotas
Territories			Revenues
			Costs
			Compensation

Figure 5–20

Budgets, forecasts, and *quotas* all have to do with planning for costs and revenues. We'll put them in their own group for now, and we'll also put *revenues, costs*, and *compensation* (a form of costs) in a group in Figure 5–21. We now have a first-pass list of global data classes, so we'll remove our higher-level generalizations of People, Place, Thing, and Event. It is not important at this point to name each group since they will evolve in the business owner's view. However, we'll give them numbers to make it easier to discuss them. We have come up with a total of fifteen global data classes for the ballpark view.

1. People	5. Places	9. Products	12. Leads
Organizations	6. Facilities	Materials	Sales Deals
2. Vendors	7. Sales Offices	WIP	Customer Purchase Orders
Purchase Orders	8. Warehouses	FGI	Sales Orders
3. Sales Reps		Parts	Shipments
Employees		10. Services	Invoices
4. Customers		11. Market Offerings	13. Service Contracts
Prospects		Prices	Service Deliveries
Markets			14. Budgets
Territories			Forecasts
			Quotas
			15. Revenues
			Costs
			Compensation

Figure 5–21

It's important not to get hung up on perfection in the ballpark view. When you exit the ballpark view, a comfortable set of ten to fifteen global data classes is a good start. Remember that we said that an enterprise is typically made up of ten to fifteen assets (or global data classes) that allow it to meet its mission. So we seem on track at this point.

Although a technique to create a ballpark view of processes and data has been defined in the last two chapters, it is not critical to follow this exact technique. The goal is to come up with a list of enterprise business functions and global data classes by using the concepts of continuity based on similarity of data. You may come up with a different technique that works better for the team that is defining your business views of the architecture.

We now move on to the business owner's view of the architecture.

The Business Owner's View

6.1 INFORMATION SYSTEMS

The business owner's view is the first level of the Zachman framework where we begin to group related processes and data together into "information systems." We are still not talking about technology. An information system is just a related set of data and processes within the enterprise. Even the dictionary defines a system as "an assemblage or combination of things or parts forming a complex or unitary whole."

Information systems, in an architected environment, encompass all processes and data that are highly related. In other words, information

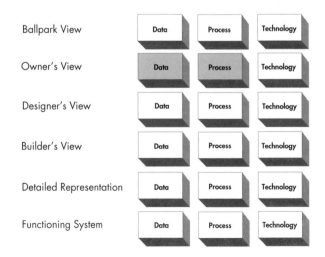

101

systems are higher-level **classes** that span processes and data. Defining clear boundaries between information systems utilizing classification theory allows for the fewest possible linkages between information systems. This, in turn, provides as much autonomy as possible between information systems development efforts when building the lower levels of the Zachman framework.

The information system autonomy provided by correctly classified architectures is what enables you to control the architecture without having to directly control all the development resources. Correctly classified information systems predetermine for the system developer what can be in or out of scope of any particular project. In other words, information systems developers must conform to the information systems boundaries or "floor plan" of the architecture when developing applications and databases further down the Zachman framework. However, they have complete autonomy within the boundaries of each information system to define *how* things are automated.

The business owner's view is a critical level of the Zachman framework. Even though the business owner's view requires more detail than the ballpark view, it is critical that business management stays heavily involved in the design of this level of the architecture. The architect cannot make the right decisions in the business owner's view without the homeowner's involvement. Defining the right boundaries between information systems is the main objective of the business views of the architecture.

The business owner's view is the master architectural plan for the enterprise. The information systems identified in this view are bounded using classification theory, not by the whim of a development team or your current organization structure. In today's environment, an application, typically with a proprietary database, is bounded by what the developers or users want in it with little thought as to how it is related to the rest of the architecture. Without the structure and control of correctly classified information systems, you get today's *dis*integrated enterprise information architectures.

To create the business owner's view of the architecture, we map our list of potential data classes to business functions to find their relationship to each other. This is called data-to-function affinity analysis in information engineering terms, affinity meaning close connection. This mapping refines the original ballpark list of global data classes along with clarifying the definitions of our enterprise business functions. Unlike the ballpark view of the architecture where we developed the data and process components separately, we will co-develop the business owner's view of the data and process architectures because we are trying to find relationships between process and data to determine information system boundaries.

6.1.1 Building the Business Owner's View

The business owner's view is more complex than the ballpark view since it deals with more detail. There are three steps to building the business owner's view.

1. For each enterprise business function, identify all the entities that it **creates** from the list of potential entities created in the ballpark view.
2. Refine the global data classes and enterprise business functions until there is a one-to-one mapping between an enterprise business function and a global data class. This mapping defines the high-level boundaries of an information system and makes it easy to communicate their scope.
3. Identify a primitive function that creates each entity within the refined global data class. This step better defines the information system in more detail by identifying the primary functions and data that should be contained within its boundaries.

6.1.2 Defining Terminology

Before we get started on the business owner's view, it's important to clarify some terminology.

There has been a lot of recent discussion, and mostly disagreement, over the terms "function," "process," and "activity," especially in organizations that have done a lot of process decomposition in support of a reengineering or total quality control (TQC) effort. These terms have a variety of meanings in the dictionary, so it is no wonder that there is disagreement on how to use them. It is not so important that we all agree on the definitions of these words as much as we understand how they are being utilized in any particular context. In the context of developing the business views of the architecture, we'll use the following definitions.

- **Function**: A high-level group of business activities. The dictionary's definition of the word "function" that is the closest to this idea is "the purpose for which something exists." This term maps to the high-level groupings of activities identified in the ballpark view as enterprise business functions. Since these are high-level groupings of activities, each enterprise business function will likely create more than one entity. We will test our enterprise business functions created in the ballpark view with this criterion. (For example, if we found that our enterprise business function of marketing creates Markets and Prospects as data classes, it would test out as a function under this definition.)

- **Primitive function**: In the upper levels of the architecture, a primitive function is still a high-level business activity. We will find these by the fact that they create a single entity. (For example, if the Lead Generation function creates Leads and no other entities, it would likely be a primitive function of the enterprise business function of marketing.)
- **Process**: A business activity. The dictionary's definition that is the closest to what we will use is "the action of going forward or on." Processes are discovered in lower levels of the Zachman framework. They create a single state of an entity and then move it forward into the next state. For example, lead qualification, a process under the primitive function Lead Generation, acts upon a lead in the unqualified state and moves it forward into the qualified state where an additional process picks it up. Since processes are determined in lower levels of the Zachman framework, we will not address them in the business views of the architecture.

6.1.3 Mapping Data to Function

We mentioned earlier that the data architecture revolves around the management of information about significant enterprise assets. Functions turn out to be similar because they manage similar assets. For example, personnel functions are similar because they primarily manage employees, a significant enterprise asset. Since functions are similar because they manage similar assets, as we break down enterprise business functions into primitive functions and the data classes that they manage, the situation shown in Figure 6–1 would make us question our original ballpark view of data or functions.

If all the primitive functions of Function A are supposed to be similar because they create similar data, then why doesn't a primitive function of Function A create the remaining Data Class 1c? The answer to these questions leads to significant business breakthroughs in the busi-

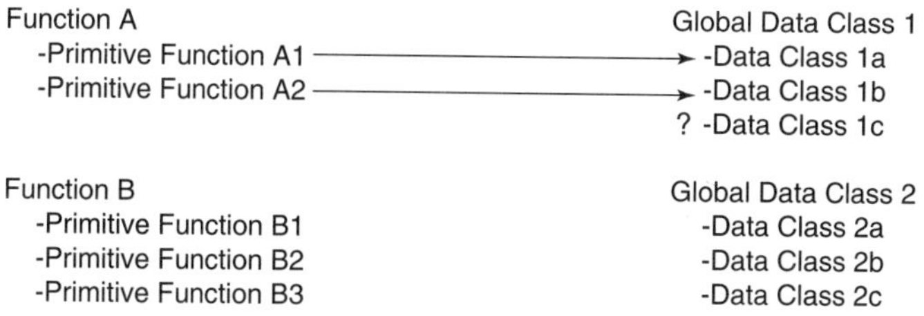

```
Function A                              Global Data Class 1
  -Primitive Function A1 ──────────────►  -Data Class 1a
  -Primitive Function A2 ──────────────►  -Data Class 1b
                                        ?  -Data Class 1c

Function B                              Global Data Class 2
  -Primitive Function B1                  -Data Class 2a
  -Primitive Function B2                  -Data Class 2b
  -Primitive Function B3                  -Data Class 2c
```

Figure 6–1
Mapping function to data class

ness owner's view of the architecture. Many, if not all, of our information disconnects in the enterprise are caused by erroneous boundaries around information systems.

The business owner's view finds the best possible boundaries for each information system based on similarities between data and functions. The method to finding the best possible boundaries for information systems is the same classification theory we have been using all along. We **classify** information systems by mapping data to function.

6.1.3.1 CRUD Matrices There is already a technique available to classify information systems. It has the unfortunate name of "CRUD matrix," where CRUD is short for **C**reate, **R**ead, **U**pdate, and **D**elete. Your information systems community may be familiar with the concept of a CRUD matrix. CRUD matrices are usually thought of as something that a systems analyst does since CRUD matrices can be created by many of the CASE tools that may be utilized in lower levels of the architecture. However, a CRUD matrix is **not** a technical matrix in the business views of the architecture.

A CRUD matrix helps you to understand where information is created in your enterprise and where it is utilized. It is the key technique used to accurately classify information systems and find their natural boundaries. A CRUD matrix is a very simple two-dimensional matrix, just like a spreadsheet, and it lists the primitive functions vertically and the entities horizontally. Each cell in the matrix identifies whether the primitive function creates, reads, updates, or deletes the corresponding entity. CRUD matrices are also utilized in lower levels of the architecture and can get very complex as primitive functions are broken down into processes and entities into database tables. But business-level CRUDs should be relatively simple.

When creating the business owner's view of the architecture, we are primarily interested in the **creation** of data. This determines the primary mapping of data to function and defines the best boundaries around information systems.

An information system, in an architected environment, will eventually consist of a suite of software applications (clients), highly integrated through the data they share, typically stored on a set of common databases (servers). Everything within an information system has to be tightly coupled.

However, information systems still need some access to data in other information systems. Even though the information system boundaries create the fewest possible links in the architecture, we will not reduce the number of links between information systems to zero.

For example, applications within the boundary of one information system may need read access to data created by another information system (Figure 6–2). They will gain this access by accessing the other information system's database servers. This is called loose coupling.

This approach of loosely coupling information systems removes all the redundancy currently found in most legacy architectures. Today's architectures are riddled with multiple copies of the same data in compatible formats because of the vertical approach to system design. In the vertical approach, many systems create data that they really need only read access to if they could get it more easily.

Completing the CRUD matrix is as easy as filling out the cells of a spreadsheet. In the CRUD matrix in Figure 6–3, PF means primitive function and ET means entity. The CRUD matrix in the figure indicates that primitive function 1 (PF1) creates entity 1 (ET1) by the C in the corresponding cell of the matrix.

The architect should take the opportunity to review any CRUD matrices that are available from other published sources or from other companies in similar industries who have completed this type of analy-

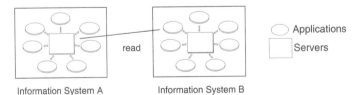

Information System A   Information System B

Figure 6–2
Gaining read access to another information system's data

	ET1	ET2	ET3	ET4	ET5	ET6	ET7	ET8	ET9
PF1	C								
PF2		C							
PF3			C						
PF4				C					
PF5					C				
PF6						C			
PF7							C		
PF8								C	
PF9									C

Figure 6–3
CRUD matrix

sis. Companies in similar industries will likely end up with very similar CRUD matrices in the business views of their architectures.

There are more business breakthroughs that can be found in the business owner's view of the architecture. Because of the additional complexity in creating the business owner view, we will create the business views of the architecture only for a subset of the enterprise—the sales and marketing functions. It is important to note, however, that all business functions must be completed before the business owner's view can be considered validated.

6.2 THE ENTERPRISE BUSINESS FUNCTION OF MARKETING

6.2.1 Step One: Identify Entities Created by the Enterprise Business Function

The enterprise business function of marketing is to "generate demand for the enterprise products and services." Step one of the business owner's view starts by examining all the potential data classes from the ballpark view and indicating which ones are likely to be *created* by the marketing function. Examples of the types of data classes that someone in the marketing department would likely select as being created by the marketing function are marked with a check mark in Figure 6–4.

6.2.2 Step Two: Resolve Groupings

You can already see that we have some problems with our ballpark view of the marketing function or with our global data classes. Since most functions (not organizations) are similar in that they act upon similar entities, why does the marketing function seem to create only one of

Figure 6–4
Data classes and entities

the six potential entities in global data class 12 and only two of four in global data class 4?

Let's start with the first question. Global data class 12 includes entities that we determined were similar because they moved a customer's need from the lead stage through the possible order, shipment, and invoicing stage. Terminology is important here. Some companies use the terms "leads" and "prospects" interchangeably, but remember, for the purposes of the architecture, we need to have clean definitions. We will define a *prospect* as a person and a *lead* as the specific need that the person has. Joe is the person and Joe's need for new stereo equipment is the lead. It is important to separate the idea of a person from the idea of a need. People obviously have more than one need in their lifetimes. It is even more important to separate these two concepts if your company is interested in installed base marketing since installed base marketing attempts to satisfy many needs for the same person over time.

In many companies, the marketing **department** is sometimes responsible for creating leads with activities such as direct mail, telemarketing, or business reply cards; however we are classifying functions and data, not organizations. We have three choices to resolve our classification problem. We can move the entity *leads* over to global data class 4 where the marketing function already creates some entities. Alternately, we can make the entity *leads* its own global data class. Or we can decide that the enterprise business function of marketing does not create the entity *leads* at all.

6.2.2.1 Breakthrough #1   Classification theory finds solutions to business problems that have plagued most enterprises for years. **Do you**

have disconnects between lead-generation activities and follow-up by the sales organization?

Lead generation, which is the likely primitive function that creates the entity *leads*, is considered a marketing process in most enterprises. But classification theory would lead us to believe it is discontinuous with the rest of the marketing function because it creates data that is more similar to data created around the sales process such as sales deals or orders. In other words, lead generation may not be a primitive marketing function at all. All of our other options don't seem to make as much sense. We could pull the entity *leads* out into a separate class by itself, but we have already determined that it is the first state of a potential order, and we shouldn't separate states of the same thing into different global data classes. We could move the entity *leads* into global data class 4, but we would have the same problem.

Our best choice is to change our view of the marketing function as the creator of the entity *leads*. Therefore, when applications supporting the marketing function start creating data beyond basic profiles about prospects and markets and start creating information about a person's specific needs (a lead), they move into the boundaries of another information system, most likely the sales information system. By eliminating this overlap, we would design an architecture that would more tightly integrate lead-generation systems with the rest of the sales systems. Without removing this overlap, you would most likely find redundancy further down the Zachman framework, such as a lead management system for the marketing function and a funnel management system for the sales function. Classification theory removes that redundancy by identifying that lead generation is not a primitive function of marketing. We will validate whether it is a primitive function of sales later, but for now we'll assume that it is no longer a primitive function of marketing.

Remember that the functions identified in the architecture do not define organization. Organizationally, you may have lead-generation activity performed by marketing departments. However, we have validated that lead-generation systems need to be provided by some other component of the architecture and **utilized** in this case by marketing departments that may be responsible for lead-generation activities.

This is an example of how classification theory and the enterprise information architecture can help business process reengineering. It would tell you that the enterprise business function of marketing starts with creating markets, prospects, and market offerings and stops before

lead generation. Most likely, the enterprise business function of sales or
what is sometimes called order acquisition starts at lead generation. We
have discovered a logical break point of discontinuity between information systems by looking at data to process affinity. To represent our decision, we remove the check mark from the entity *leads* and move on to
resolving the remaining issues for the marketing function.

Now we need to resolve why the marketing function creates only
two of four entities in global data class 4.

6.2.2.2 Breakthrough #2   Do you have a disconnect between marketing's view of market segments and the setting of sales territories?

As part of generating demand for products and services, the
marketing function (not necessarily the marketing organization) creates
data about target markets. For example, a target market for a particular
product line might be electronic manufacturing companies over $50 mil-
lion in annual sales. Think of these types of generic target markets as the
planning phase of more specific markets. The more specific target markets are the actual prospects, in this case the electronic manufacturing
companies, that fit the target market criteria. If you take this viewpoint,
it validates that markets and prospects belong in the same global data
class.

Do territories belong in the same global data class? Aren't sales territories really just a group of prospects? They are very similar to the idea
of a target market, but just a little more specific. For example, let's say
that we have identified a target market of electronic manufacturing companies with over $50 million in annual sales. We also have identified a
list of all the prospective companies that fit that criterion. Sales territories would then just be the subsetting of those companies assigned to a
sales rep or sales channel. Since we are still working with the same data,

it makes sense to keep all of these entities in the same global data class. Therefore, if the marketing function creates markets and prospects, it should also create sales territories.

Again, organizationally, you may decide to have your sales **organization** create sales territories, but the architecture groups the primitive function that creates sales territories with the rest of the primitive functions that generate target markets and prospects. Further down the Zachman framework, this decision would require that applications that create or manage sales territories be highly integrated with applications that manage target markets and prospects. We'll reflect that decision by indicating that the entity *territories* is created by the marketing function.

We have one more problem to resolve. There is a remaining entity, *customers*, in global data class 4 that we don't think the marketing function creates. First, let's succinctly define customers as those people who have already purchased from us. We originally thought that the entity *customers* is just a different state of prospect. If they are truly states of the same thing, we should put them in the same group. On the other hand, it doesn't seem like the marketing function should be the creator of the entity *customers* since we earlier decided that the marketing function ends before creating leads, the first stage before becoming a customer through an actual order. The entity *customers* seems much more continuous with the concept of an order which will probably be created by the sales function. In fact, earlier we grouped internal purchase orders with the role of vendor for the same reason. Because we haven't yet discussed the sales function, we will make the entity *customers* its own global data class for now and test our theory when we analyze the sales function.

1. People	5. Places	9. Products	12. Leads
Organizations	6. Facilities	Materials	Sales Deals
2. Vendors	7. Sales Offices	WIP	Customer Purchase Orders
Purchase Orders	8. Warehouses	FGI	Sales Orders
3. Sales Reps		Parts	Shipments
Employees		10. Services	Invoices
4. Prospects ✓		11. Market Offerings ✓	13. Service Contracts
Markets ✓		Prices ✓	Service Deliveries
Territories ✓			14. Budgets
4a. Customers			Forecasts
			Quotas
			15. Revenues
			Costs
			Compensation

Since we already indicated that the marketing function creates both *market offerings* and *prices*, global data class 11 seems to belong to the marketing function. We already resolved many of the issues in this area when we separated products and services from market offerings and prices in the ballpark view.

We have now refined our mapping of data to function. We have two validated global data classes that map to the marketing function.

Now we need to refine our ballpark view with the modifications we have made in the business owner's view. First we'll name our new and improved global data classes that will replace the original ballpark view. The easiest way to name these validated global data classes is to select one of the entity names that best represents what is in the class. However, new names can be given if that makes it easier to communicate the ballpark view. In our case, we have highlighted the entity that we will also use as the name for the ballpark view data class. For example, we'll use the term Markets to refer in the ballpark view to global data class 4 and Market Offerings to refer to global data class 11. Notice that it isn't necessary to name the ballpark view data classes until they have been validated in the business owner's view.

1. People	5. Places	9. Products	12. Leads
Organizations	6. Facilities	Materials	Sales Deals
2. Vendors	7. Sales Offices	WIP	Customer Purchase Orders
Purchase Orders	8. Warehouses	FGI	Sales Orders
3. Sales Reps		Parts	Shipments
Employees		10. Services	Invoices
4. Prospects ✓		11. **Market Offerings** ✓	13. Service Contracts
Markets ✓		Prices ✓	Service Deliveries
Territories ✓			14. Budgets
4a. Customers			Forecasts
			Quotas
			15. Revenues
			Costs
			Compensation

Each of our two global data classes created by the marketing function has more than one entity in it. We said earlier that a function likely creates more than one entity, so certainly marketing is validated as a function versus a primitive function. To make it easier to communicate the business views of the architecture, it is helpful to have a one-to-one mapping between the global data classes (each containing more than one entity) and an enterprise business function. For that reason, we will break the original enterprise business function of marketing down into two enterprise business functions, each mapped to one of our two global data classes.

Let's call these two refined enterprise business functions "product development," which creates the global data class Market Offerings, and "target marketing," which creates the global data class Markets. We now have a one-to-one mapping between global data class and enterprise business function, which will make it easier to communicate the business views.

6.2.3 Step Three: Identify Primitive Functions for Each Entity

In order to better describe the business owner's view of the architecture, we include the next level of detail which is the actual entities and primitive functions included within the validated global data class and enterprise business function. Since we already know the entities within our two global data classes, we will now identify a primitive function that creates each entity. For the sake of simplicity, we will identify only creating functions. There are other marketing functions that are primarily readers of data. For example, the creation of a direct mailing list would require read access to prospect profiles in order to select a target audience. It is not important to identify read-only functions in the business owner's view since they don't impact the overall architecture. Primitive functions are easily identified by looking at each entity. Figures 6–5 and 6–6 show first-pass matrices identifying primitive functions and entities for each enterprise function.

Primitive Function/Data	Markets	Territories	Prospects
Identify Target Markets	C		
Identify Sales Potential within Markets		C	
Identify Prospects			C

Figure 6–5
Primitive functions that create entities for target marketing

Primitive Function/Data	Market Offering	Prices
Create Market Offerings	C	
Price Market Offerings		C

Figure 6–6
Primitive functions that create entities for product development

Each of these matrices identifies the boundaries of two information systems we'll call the target marketing information system and the product development information system. Remember that we are using the term "system" differently. These systems will consist of a set of applications (clients) and databases (servers) that cover the functionality and data needs defined in the CRUD matrix. These information system names obviously don't roll off the tongue as well as we'd like, so of course we need to come up with some cute acronyms, one of the most important tasks of any new system design project. We'll leave that up to the reader.

For the original ballpark enterprise business function of marketing, we now have defined two information systems. The ballpark view of these information systems is defined by listing the new enterprise business function and its global data class as follows:

Corrected Ballpark View of the Target Marketing Information System

Enterprise business function	*Global data class*
Target marketing	Markets

Corrected Ballpark View of the Product Development Information System

Enterprise business function	*Global data class*
Product Development	Market Offerings

The business owner's view of these information systems is defined using the CRUD matrices in the figures indicating the actual entities and primitive functions that are included within each information system's boundaries.

6.3 CROSS-FUNCTIONAL DATA CLASSES

Before we move on to the sales function, we need to discuss some general data classes that do not belong to any specific business function. Earlier, we identified prospects as a role that an organization or person can play.

The entity *prospects* would have prospect-oriented data about organizations or persons such as competitive products that they own, interests, and so on. The entity *people* would have the master data about people such as their names and phone numbers that are not specific to their role as a prospect or customer. Remember that organizations and persons can play other roles such as vendors, and that is why we separated out the entities *organizations* and *people* into their own class. However, what is the enterprise business function that would actually create the entities *people* and *organizations*?

It turns out that we will need to identify a more generic enterprise business function that creates these cross-functional entities, although the roles that these entities can play can be isolated to a single business function. For example, we have identified that marketing creates the role of prospect, and it is likely that the procurement function creates the role of vendor. However, both functions would need the ability to create a new person or organization if it did not already exist. Therefore, classification theory tells us to pull it out as a separate function.

We can consider the global data classes that do not belong to a specific business function to be cross-functional reference data or master data for the enterprise. In the architecture, the master data and the processes that create master data form their own information systems. We'll name the global data class that contains the master entities *person* and *organization* the Organizations global data class.

This new global data class, along with primitive functions that create the master entities *organization* and *person*, make up an information system that we'll call the organization master information system. We'll call the enterprise business function that creates this master data "organization master data management." There will likely also be a few more

1. People	5. Places	9. Products	12. Leads
Organizations	6. Facilities	Materials	Sales Deals
2. Vendors	7. Sales Offices	WIP	Customer Purchase Orders
Purchase Orders	8. Warehouses	FGI	Sales Orders
3. Sales Reps		Parts	Shipments
Employees		10. Services	Invoices
4. Prospects ✓		11. **Market Offerings** ✓	13. Service Contracts
Markets ✓		Prices ✓	Service Deliveries
Territories ✓			14. Budgets
4a. Customers			Forecasts
			Quotas
			15. Revenues
			Costs
			Compensation

master information systems as the rest of the architecture is fleshed out
such as potentially a "places master information system." The creating
functions in these master information systems are invoked by applications in many other information systems. For example, in order to create
a prospect with an application that is part of the target marketing information system, the application would need to invoke an application that
is part of the organization master information system to create the person or organization data if it did not already exist.

Therefore, we'll create the CRUD matrix for one additional information system (see Figure 6–7).

Primitive Function/Data	Organizations	People
Create Organizations	C	
Create People		C

Figure 6–7
Organization master information system

The ballpark view of this information system is defined as follows:

Enterprise business function   *Global data class*

Organization master data management   Organizations

We have now completed both the ballpark and business owner's
view of the original marketing function.

6.4 THE ENTERPRISE FUNCTION OF SALES

6.4.1 Step One: Identify Entities Created by the Enterprise Business Function

The enterprise business function of sales picks up where the marketing function left off. In the ballpark view, we defined the sales func-

tion as "obtaining agreements from customers to purchase products and services." Right off the bat, we'd better correct this statement to reflect our more succinct definition of customer as one who has already purchased from us. A more precise definition of the sales function would now be "to obtain agreements from prospects to purchase products and services." After creating the business owner's view of the marketing function, we now think that the sales function starts with a person's need (lead) and attempts to transition that need into an order (potentially through a quotation state for more complex businesses). The following check marks indicate the likely entities that a sales manager might select as being created by the sales function.

6.4.2 Step Two: Resolve Groupings

We have some problems to resolve since we don't think that the sales function creates all the potential entities in each global data class. Let's start with global data class 12. We have indicated that we don't think the sales function creates shipments and invoices. If we were building the business owner's view of all enterprise business functions, it would be more likely that the enterprise business function of distribution creates the shipment. In addition, a shipment is a physical thing, unlike the rest of class 12. If we agree with these viewpoints, we need to pull the entity *shipments* out as discontinuous with global data class 12. We'll number this new class 12a. It will need to be validated in the analysis of other enterprise business functions.

But what about the entity invoices? It seems like it's the same data as the order information.

6.4.2.1 Breakthrough #3 **Do your customers have trouble matching their purchase orders to your sales orders and invoices?** Most companies think of a customer purchase order as just an

1. People	5. Places	9. Products	12. Leads ✓
Organizations	6. Facilities	Materials	Sales Deals ✓
2. Vendors	7. Sales Offices	WIP	Customer Purchase Orders ✓
Purchase Orders	8. Warehouses	FGI	Sales Orders ✓
3. Sales Reps ✓		Parts	Invoices
Employees		10. Services	12a.Shipments
4. Prospects		11. Market Offerings	13. Service Contracts
Markets		Prices	Service Deliveries
Territories			14. Budgets
4a.Customers ✓			Forecasts ✓
			Quotas ✓
			15. Revenues
			Costs
			Compensation

attribute of their internal sales order. In other words, they create their own internal sales order, and somewhere on that sales order they list the customer's purchase order number. However, by classifying customer purchase orders, sales orders, and invoices together in the same global data class, it makes us look at their similarity.

Isn't our sales order just the internal view of a customer's purchase order? If they are in fact the same thing, we should have just a single entity to represent both views. Which one should stay?

Well, the customer's purchase order happens before a sales order. If we use the customer's purchase order as the entity representing both the customer's view and our internal view of the order, it would lead us in lower levels of the architecture to identity the entity using the customer's purchase order number, which would follow it through its life cycle until invoicing. In other words, there would not be something called a sales order number at all. **The customer's purchase order number would be your sales order number because they are the same thing!** All your internal paperwork like packing lists and invoices would match the customer's purchase order automatically. This is the type of business value one gets from correct data classification.

There is one practical issue to resolve if we use the customer's purchase order number to identify the customer's purchase order and move it through its life cycle. There is the potential that multiple customers might use the same numbering scheme for purchase orders. This could make it difficult to uniquely identify a particular customer purchase order within your company.

However, if we modeled this area, the data model would show a key relationship between the entity *customer purchase order* and the entity *customer*. When we build a database in lower levels of the architecture, the entity *customer purchase order* becomes a data table with a key of purchase order number. The entity *customer* becomes a data table with a key of customer number. These tables are linked together because they have a relationship. The link is provided in the database by carrying the key of customer number in the customer purchase order table. In the customer purchase order table, the customer number key concatenated or added to the customer's purchase order number makes the number unique in your company.

For example, we would use 50-PO30000 to uniquely identify customer number 50's purchase order number PO30000 with PO30000 being the order number from **their** purchasing system. In physical data structures, represented by the data model below, relationships become keys between data tables (entities become data tables, eventually). Therefore, in the entity *purchase order*, there is already both the customer number and the purchase order number.

The model in Figure 6–8 indicates that there is no such entity as sales order. However, the entity *customer purchase order* would probably collect a few extra fields of data as it moves through the order processing process such as our internal receipt or acceptance date. This viewpoint gives an outward looking customer orientation to this part of the architecture. The customer becomes the focal point for the order, not our internal paperwork. To support this viewpoint, we'll remove the entity *sales order* from the Customer Purchase Order global data class, and we'll also include the entity *invoice* as being part of the data that is created by the sales function. Note that the creation of the invoice is included in this global data class but not the collection of the receivable, which is likely to be part of the revenue entity. We'll call global data class 12 customer purchase order.

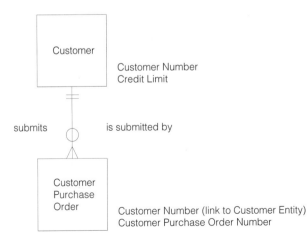

Figure 6–8

1. People	5. Places	9. Products	12. Leads ✓
Organizations	6. Facilities	Materials	Sales Deals ✓
2. Vendors	7. Sales Offices	WIP	**Customer Purchase Orders** ✓
Purchase Orders	8. Warehouses	FGI	Invoices ✓
3. Sales Reps ✓		Parts	12a.Shipments
Employees		10. Services	13. Service Contracts
4. Prospects		11. **Market Offerings**	Service Deliveries
Markets		Prices	14. Budgets
Territories			Forecasts ✓
4a.Customers ✓			Quotas ✓
			15. Revenues
			Costs
			Compensation

We'll now move on to resolving the problem in global data class 14. We have identified that the sales function creates sales forecasts and quotas, but not budgets.

6.4.2.2 Breakthrough #4   Do you have a problem with integrated planning such as integrating sales forecasting and demand planning for manufacturing? Again classification theory helps us with a sticky wicket.

Classification theory tells us that **forecasting and quota setting are not primitive sales functions**. (Remember not to confuse organization with function.) Since the process of forecasting and quota setting needs to happen as part of many enterprise business functions such as demand planning for manufacturing, hiring plans for personnel, and sales forecasting and quota setting for sales, classification theory says it can't belong to only one of these functions and must be pulled out as a separate business function. It may belong with the finance and administrative function from our original list of enterprise business functions, or we may want to create a new enterprise business function called planning. All we know is that classification theory has to resolve this redundancy. Since we aren't discussing any of the other enterprise business functions, we will identify only that the entities *forecasts* and *quota* do not belong to the sales function. They will likely have continuity with the rest of the entities in global data class 14, so we'll leave them there for now. It is likely that additional planning-oriented entities will end up in this global data class. By identifying the similarities in these entities, eventually an information system will be created that will integrate planning across the enterprise.

Therefore, we remove the check marks from global data class 14 since they are not created by the sales function. Remember that function and organization are different. It is perfectly all right to have the sales

organization utilize the planning information system to do sales forecasting and quota setting, but now those activities will be integrated with the rest of the planning functions in the enterprise.

Here are our global data class groupings for the sales function at this point.

6.4.2.3 **Breakthrough #5**   Although we have indicated that forecasts and quotas are not created by the sales function and are most likely created by some sort of planning information system that will integrate forecasting across functions, there is another hidden breakthrough in this area. It has to do with increasing the accuracy of the sales forecast itself.

Do you have a problem with accurate order forecasting information?

As we've discussed before, in most enterprises, current systems are typically vertically mapped to departments. Therefore leads are typically managed in marketing systems; active sales deals are managed in funnel management systems; customer orders and quotes are managed in order processing systems. Then we usually have a sales forecasting system and demand planning system on top of all that redundancy. Of course, in most companies, none of these systems are integrated. Therefore, it is extremely difficult to pull together even a monthly view of the sales forecast, much less an hourly or daily view which is probably what is needed for effective resource management. At any one point, an active sales situation could be in a lead generation system, funnel management system, order management system, sales forecasting system, demand planning system for manufacturing, or all five. No wonder we can't make any sense of it!

We have assumed that global data class 14 will eventually identify the need for a planning information system that will have the capability to integrate plans across the enterprise. But many of those plans need access to accurate lead and order data to create a good forecast of future resources needed. But the planning system should not have to re-create this information; those entities are created by the order acquisition system in the Customer Purchase Orders data class as we've recently discussed.

The Customer Purchase Orders data class solves our problem of feeding integrated and accurate lead and order data to our planning processes. As shown in Figure 6–9, this is accomplished by gaining read access from the planning information system to the order acquisition system. The order acquisition system now contains the Customer Purchase Order data class which has integrated information about leads, deals, and orders.

This type of architecture would allow for plans to be updated by the minute if required, as opposed to the laborious monthly demand planning or forecasting process that most companies go through to consolidate and make sense of all the duplicate data. In our new Customer Purchase Order data class, information about the lead would flow through the sales cycle, perhaps as a quote first and then eventually as an order, with no duplication of effort even if there were multiple applications in the information system, greatly increasing the accuracy of this data. Of course, at any point in the cycle, the sales situation could be canceled and deleted from the information system (and, therefore, the sales forecast) or kept as historical marketing information.

Oh, no! Not that closed-loop marketing stuff again! Don't tell me that the marketing department is going to make me follow up on those terrible leads they send me! Remember that classification theory has told us that lead generation is a primitive **sales** function, not a marketing function. That means it has to be tightly integrated with the rest of the primitive sales functions. In the architecture, this will eventually mean

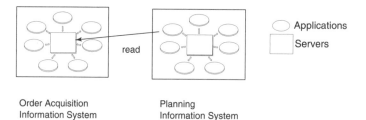

Order Acquisition   Planning
Information System   Information System

Figure 6–9
Accessing accurate sales forecasts from the planning information system

that lead generation would be automated through the systems that support the rest of the sales processes. This would allow, for example, lead-generation activities to identify whether a sales rep wants or needs leads to start with. In many companies today, leads are generated in marketing systems without concern for the status of the sales rep funnels or even the availability of a sales rep to follow up. For example, leads are sent to sales reps who have more than enough to work on already and don't have time to follow up on additional leads. Other sales reps with empty sales funnels may not get any leads at all. It is interesting that this type of integration has been called closed-loop marketing. With our current definitions, classification theory would tell us that it should be called closed-loop selling.

Remember, while lead generation is classified as a primitive sales function, it does not mean that lead-generation activities can't occur in a marketing organization such as an inside telemarketing organization, but the systems and processes that create leads must be tightly integrated with the other primitive functions of sales. And the information that is provided by this tightly integrated information system must be accessible to the planning functions automated in another information system that revolves around global data class 14.

Now we'll go back to our current list of entities. Next, we'll validate whether the entity *customers*, pulled out into its own global data class when we looked at the marketing function, is really created by the sales function.

1. People	5. Places	9. Products	12. Leads	✓
Organizations	6. Facilities	Materials	Sales Deals	✓
2. Vendors	7. Sales Offices	WIP	**Customer Purchase Orders**	✓
Purchase Orders	8. Warehouses	FGI	Invoices	✓
3. Sales Reps ✓		Parts	12a.Shipments	✓
Employees		10. Services	13. Service Contracts	
4. Prospects		11. **Market Offerings**	Service Deliveries	
Markets		Prices	14. Budgets	
Territories			Forecasts	
Customers			Quotas	
			15. Revenues	
			Costs	
			Compensation	

6.4.2.4 Breakthrough #6   Some companies view a person (or organization) as either a customer or a prospect, but not both. With this viewpoint, a prospect transitions to a customer once he or she has placed an order. This data model implies that, once someone buys from you, you are no longer going to treat that person as a prospect. However, for most enterprises, except perhaps a funeral home, past customers are the most likely future purchasers.

We need to clean up our definition of customer. We know that a customer of one product could be a prospect for another product. It is also likely that a customer of one product can be a prospect for a replacement item for the same product. Therefore, a more precise definition of a customer has to do with the customer's relationship to a **line item on a particular order**. Stay with me now.

One way of looking at the difference between a customer and a prospect is this: If your company sells hats, gloves, and coats and a person has purchased hats and gloves from you, he or she would be a customer for hats and gloves and a prospect for coats. However, if you broaden that perspective, the whole concept of customer goes away since even the customers of hats and gloves are probably immediate prospects for additional or replacement hats and gloves at some point. This viewpoint is an important business breakthrough.

The concept of customer is much like the concept of sales order. The original entity *customer* is really just those additional elements of data that you capture about a prospect for administering an order, such as credit rating or taxability. In fact, if you really did intend for a prospect to order from you only once (perhaps if you sell fraudulent securities), this type of data would clearly be considered part of the order, and you wouldn't even want to keep information about the ongoing relationship with you as a customer. For this reason, the entity *customer* belongs with the rest of the prospect-oriented entities in global data class 4 rather than being its own class. This also means that crediting the additional elements of data about a prospect necessary to accept an order is part of the target marketing information system. So, we'll remove the checkmark from the customer entity and place it back with global class 4.

1. People	5. Places	9. Products	12. Leads	✓
Organizations	6. Facilities	Materials	Sales Deals	✓
2. Vendors	7. Sales Offices	WIP	**Customer Purchase Orders**	✓
Purchase Orders	8. Warehouses	FGI	Invoices	✓
3. Sales Reps ✓		Parts	12a. Shipments	✓
Employees		10. Services	13. Service Contracts	
4. Prospects		11. **Market Offerings**	Service Deliveries	
Markets		Prices	14. Budgets	
Territories			Forecasts	
Customers			Quotas	
			15. Revenues	
			Costs	
			Compensation	

We now need to resolve the remaining problem with global data class 3. We have indicated that we create only one of the two entities in that class.

6.4.2.5 Breakthrough #7   Most companies think that the role of sales reps is played only by their employees such as an internal sales force. However, this reduces your architecture's flexibility to support the ability to expand easily into different sales channels outside your enterprise. Sales reps in other sales channels play a similar role—sales rep. If we group the role of sales rep with the role of employee, our architecture would make it difficult to treat external sales reps the same as internal sales reps. If you pull the role of sales rep out separately, the architecture would support treating internal and external sales channels the same. For example, the architecture would enable you to pay commissions or assign territories to both internal and external sales reps.

There certainly is at least one difference between an internal sales rep and an external sales rep. That would be captured in the relationship between the person and the organization they report to, in one case your company, in another case, another company. In most companies, our vertical mentality dramatically separates our view of sales reps as employees from our view of sales reps playing a role in an alternate sales channel. This myopic data classification scheme creates huge departmental and information system separations between sales channels, making it difficult to react quickly to the marketplace. We'll go back to data modeling to show the vast difference between the two approaches. We'll assume in the models in Figure 6–10 that a sales rep can have only one sales territory but that a sales territory can be covered by more than one sales rep.

The data model on the right allows any person, employee or not, to be assigned to a sales territory. This model would link entities like *commission* to the role of a sales rep, a role that could be played by anyone, and makes the architecture flexible enough to deal with all kinds of sales channels in the future. The model on the left limits your architecture to internal sales reps as your only sales channel.

If we adopt the viewpoint of the data model on the right, we need to separate the sales reps and employees entities. In the architecture, this would mean that the role of sales rep (such as commission management) is not automated within the personnel information system. Other related entities such as *commission* would most likely be included with the sales rep class. We'll create a new global data class numbered 3a to separate

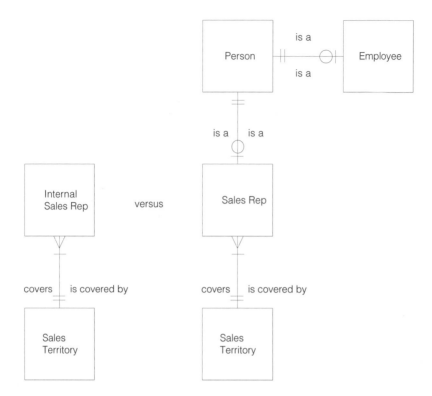

Figure 6–10

the entity *employees* from the entity *sales reps* and add *commission* as an
entity grouped with *sales reps*. We'll call global data class 3 Sales Reps.

1. People	5. Places	9. Products	12. Leads ✓
Organizations	6. Facilities	Materials	Sales Deals ✓
2. Vendors	7. Sales Offices	WIP	**Customer Purchase Orders** ✓
Purchase Orders	8. Warehouses	FGI	Invoices ✓
3. **Sales Reps** ✓		Parts	12a.Shipments ✓
Commission ✓		10. Services	13. Service Contracts
3a.Employees		11. **Market Offerings**	Service Deliveries
4. Prospects		Prices	14. Budgets
Markets			Forecasts
Territories			Quotas
Customers			15. Revenues
			Costs
			Compensation

We now have resolved all of our classification problems for the enterprise business function of sales. We've identified two global data classes—Sales Reps and Customer Purchase Orders—that are owned by the sales function. As before, with the enterprise business function of marketing, we should take the opportunity to break up the enterprise business function of sales into two new enterprise business functions that map to their created global data classes. We'll call these two new functions sales channel management and order acquisition. The corrected ballpark view of the sales function is as follows:

Enterprise business function	*Global data class*
Order acquisition	Customer Purchase Orders
Sales channel management	Sales Reps

6.4.3 Step Three: Identify Primitive Functions for Each Entity

In order to complete the business owner's view, we need to identify a primitive function for each entity within each global data class. The primitive functions and entities for each new business function identified in the CRUD matrix in Figure 6–11 comprise two new information systems.

Order Acquisition

Data/Primitive Function	Leads	Sales Deals	Customer Purchase Orders
Generate Leads	C		
Qualify Leads		C	
Generate Purchase Orders			C

Sales Channel Management

Data/Primitive Function	Sales Reps	Commission
Determine Sales Channel	C	
Pay Commission		C

Figure 6–11
Order acquisition and sales channel management matrices

6.5 ENTERPRISE ARCHITECTURE STANDARDS

With the completion of a set of information systems for the enterprise, we have defined our first set of standards for the architecture. Remember that standards increase our flexibility by decoupling components from one another. The boundaries of our information systems become enterprise standards and developers must conform to them. These information system boundaries are the floor plan of the architecture and cannot be changed by the whim of a user or development team.

6.6 INFORMATION ENGINEERING TERMINOLOGY

If you are familiar with the concepts of information engineering, you may have heard of the term "business areas." Business areas are created by the same data to process affinity analysis that we just completed and are equivalent to our concept of information systems.

You may also have heard the term "subject area." Subject areas are high-level groupings of data and can be considered equivalent to both our global data classes and our entities. Both of those groups of data are still fairly high level. In lower levels of the architecture, our entities will break down into multiple entities that will eventually become tables in a database as systems are designed and created.

6.7 COMPLETING THE BUSINESS VIEW OF THE ARCHITECTURE

We have completed the business owner's view of the marketing and sales functions. However, there are probably many more breakthroughs that can be found when completing the rest of the enterprise business functions. For example, when creating the business owner's view of procurement, you would have to look at the similarity between internal purchase orders that you send to a vendor and the purchase orders that you receive from your customers. After all, didn't we already determine that the customer's purchase order is the same as what we thought of as our sales order? Food for thought.

It is not the intent of this chapter to provide the business owner's view for all functions of any particular company, only to provide examples of how to build the view and how it can provide business breakthroughs for your enterprise. In fact, by not completing the business views of all enterprise business functions, it is likely that additional redundancy has not yet been removed in these examples of the sales and marketing functions.

6.8 DATA MODELS FOR THE BUSINESS VIEWS OF THE ARCHITECTURE

Although none of our steps to building the business views of the architecture has included completing an enterprise data model, it is a requirement. The architecture team has the option of completing an enterprise data model as the last step of each business view or waiting until both business views have been completed and then creating the enterprise data model for both views. The second option is sometimes better because business people, who are typically unfamiliar with the concept of data modeling, can be overwhelmed by attempting to data model the entire enterprise, even at high levels of abstraction such as the business views. In addition, it is only after completing the business views that most business people understand the importance of data and are willing to complete an enterprise data model. Since our goal is only to come to a conclusion about information systems boundaries, it is possible to accomplish that goal by discussing entities and data-to-function mapping without enterprise data models being completed first. However, data models do need to be completed before you can consider the business views of the architecture finished.

As mentioned before, the data modeling that we do as part of the business views of the architecture are at a much higher level of abstraction than the data modeling activities that occur in the subsequent levels of the architecture. Most historical enterprise data models provide too much detail for easy comprehension by business people, the target audience of the business views. In fact, in order to data model an entire enterprise, a rather high level of abstraction is necessary to avoid overwhelming the modeling team itself, regardless of how technical it is. For this reason, very high-level data models—what could be called the mission data model and global data model—are utilized as representations of the two business views. As further levels of the architecture are developed, in most cases it only makes sense to create detailed data models for a single information system at a time. It may never make sense to represent the lowest-level data model for the entire enterprise, since even Einstein would probably get a headache trying to comprehend it.

Although the architect has the option of delaying the creation of the business views of the enterprise data models, it is important to deliver data models for each business view. These abstract data models are critical communication tools for the rest of the enterprise.

6.8.1 Mission Data Models

The mission data model is a high-level data representation of the mission of the enterprise. It should be a deliverable of the ballpark view, but again it is sometimes more easily completed after the business team has gone through the first two levels of the architecture and has a better understanding of the importance of the data architecture. The mission data model, in essence, takes the nouns out of the mission statement of an enterprise. For example, if the mission statement of an enterprise is to manufacture, sell, and support products that meet the needs of its target markets, one might come up with a mission data model like the one shown in Figure 6–12 (nouns are products, needs, markets).[1]

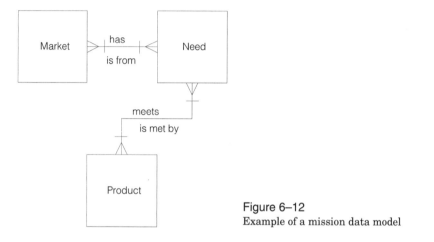

Figure 6–12
Example of a mission data model

This mission model suggests that markets have one or many needs that can be met by one or many products. The important business view highlighted by this particular mission model is that products satisfy the needs of markets. This would lead one to emphasize an architecture that is very focused on understanding the needs of markets since the concept of order and, therefore, revenue growth is hidden in the line between needs and products. A more popular mission model, but one that misses this viewpoint, might look like that shown in Figure 6–13.

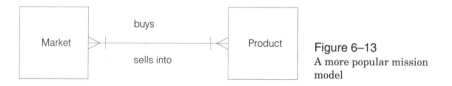

Figure 6–13
A more popular mission model

This model identifies that there are products and markets in which those products are sold. Without the concept of needs, however, this mission model misses the importance of understanding the changing needs

1. Finkelstein, Clive, *Strategic Systems Development*, Singapore: Addison-Wesley Publishing Company, 1992, pp. 162–3.

of the enterprise's target markets. An airline may today sell many of its most profitable seats to the business traveler as a target market. With the more needs-focused model, one might start thinking about additional products, such as video conferencing, that this enterprise or, more importantly, another competing enterprise can provide to meet the needs of business travelers.

Mission data models, in addition to providing a framework for the information architecture at its highest level, usually spark creative discussion on the future of the enterprise itself. For that reason alone, they are extremely important.

6.8.2 Global Data Models

The global data model is a deliverable of the business owner's view. Again, it is sometimes helpful to wait until this point to create it since we have modified and validated our global data classes through our work in levels one and two. Once we have a valid set of global data classes, we draw the actual ERD to create the global data model for the enterprise. Since we have not yet validated the global data classes for all the enterprise business functions (just sales and marketing), we can't yet draw the global data model for our example enterprise. However, Figure 6–14 illustrates a draft of a piece of the global data model representing four of our global data classes.

Our global data model for the sales and marketing functions seems to miss the concept of market needs captured in the mission data model. The model in Figure 6–14 does indicate that purchase orders for our market offerings are submitted by markets. But it doesn't capture the

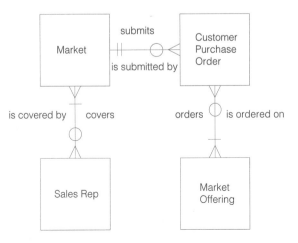

Figure 6–14
Part of global data model representing sales and marketing

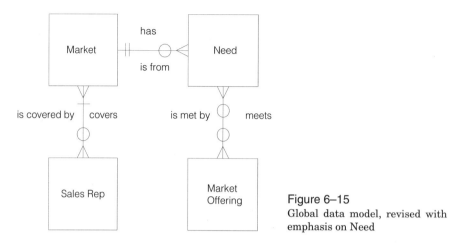

Figure 6–15
Global data model, revised with
emphasis on Need

essence of a successful business—that its market offerings meet the
needs of markets and that is why purchase orders are submitted. This is
because, in the business owner's view, we decided to call the global data
class that included leads (needs) and their follow-on stages of orders
Customer Purchase Orders. This term doesn't capture our mission
model's emphasis on needs. Since the audience of the global data model
is business people, it would probably make sense to rename that particular global data class so that the intent of the mission model is not lost.
If you rename that global data class Need rather than Customer Purchase Order, then the global data model better matches our mission
model.

We had to make a small but important change in the relationship
between the global data class Need and Market Offering. That relationship is now optional. In other words, it has gone from one to many to zero
to many. A customer purchase order has to have at least one market
offering on it or it wouldn't be submitted to anyone. However, a customer
need does not have to be met by any current market offering, in your
business or any other. Mission and global data models are *business* models, not technology models. This model emphasizes that business opportunity and customer satisfaction are found by clearly understanding the
customer's needs.

6.8.3 Logical and Conceptual ERDs

The terms logical and conceptual data model are more applicable to
lower levels of the architecture. At the lower levels of the architecture
such as the designer's and builder's views, developers are usually dealing

with a single information system. With this less abstract view, data models move from representing high-level entities or subject areas to entities that eventually become database tables. For example, the entity *prospect* might be represented by entities *prospect, competitive product profile, recent marketing activity,* and so on. It is not important for the business manager to understand the level of detail necessary to build a database, but the mission and global data models and the information system definitions must be conformed to by conceptual and logical data models created by information systems designers.

We now have completed an example of the business views of the data and process architectures within the Zachman framework.

The Business Views of the Technology Architecture

The business views of the architecture define a suite of information systems that meets all of the data and process needs in the enterprise. These information system boundaries allow us to partition or "chunk" the architecture down into systems that are reasonably autonomous and have the fewest possible linkages between them. Once we've established the boundaries for these information systems in the business views of the architecture, they can be delegated to development teams who can design or purchase information systems with reasonable autonomy. This is how you control the overall architecture without requiring central development.

However, so far we have identified only which information system should *create* each data class. When we complete the remaining consonants of the CRUD matrix (read, update, and delete) further down in the Zachman framework, we will find that most data is still primarily accessed and managed within the information system that creates it. However, we will also find that most information systems still need limited access to some data created in other information systems. Our suite of information systems has the minimum number of links between systems, but this number is not zero.

So far, we have developed the business views of the process and data architectures of the Zachman framework. Earlier we said that technology changes so rapidly that the technology column of the Zachman framework is not stable. Therefore, the technology column isn't really worth worrying about in the business views where we are setting long-term strategy. However, there is still some business guidance that we need to provide to the technology experts who will be defining the technology architecture.

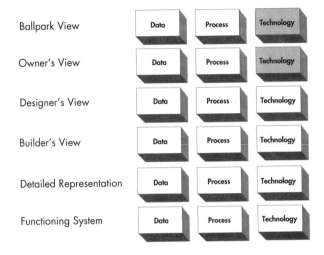

Data and processes *within* information system boundaries can be considered tightly coupled. Data and processes *between* information systems can be considered loosely coupled. There is some guidance we can give to the technology community about how to loosely couple information systems together so that they can access each other's data without re-creating the spaghetti architecture we have today.

Let's start with what we have defined so far in the business views. If we were to draw a simple picture of the business views of the technology architecture, it would consist of our five information systems plus the other information systems that will eventually be identified after analysis of the rest of the enterprise business functions.

In Figure 7–1, each box represents an information system containing a tightly integrated set of software and data that automates all the primitive functions scoped within the information system. Note that technology isn't important in this particular picture. We could be using anything from legacy terminal-to-host applications with indexed files all the way to the latest and greatest client/server or object-oriented systems. The important point about this picture is that everything within the boundaries of the information system must be tightly integrated.

The classification process that we went through to find our informa-

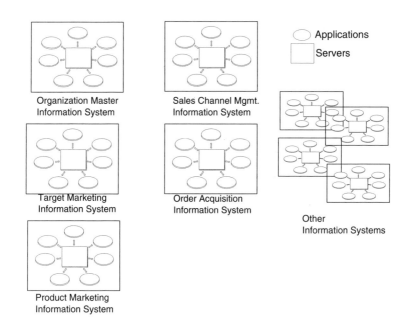

Figure 7–1
Enterprise information systems

tion system boundaries reduced the number of linkages we will need between information systems. However, that number is not zero. For example, one or more of the applications within our order acquisition information system will need access to prospect data that we have determined is created within the target marketing information system. It is also likely that somehow the orders from the order acquisition system need to be scheduled against planned inventory or finished goods inventory (FGI), which is most likely created in the production or manufacturing information system. We'll draw links between the information systems to indicate the business views of these information system links in the technology architecture (see Figure 7–2).

7.1 ARCHITECTURE COMPLICATIONS IN LARGE COMPANIES

In the simplest possible case, a small company may want to have the technology architecture illustrated in Figure 7–2, which indicates that applications within one information system would directly access another information system's database where necessary. The illustration also implies that each information system would have a single database and multiple applications accessing it. Sound a little too easy?

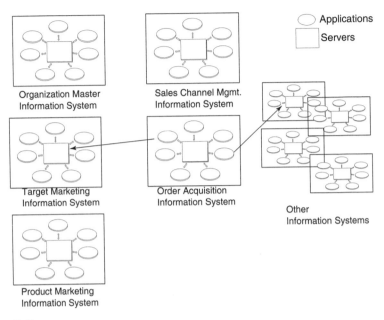

Organization Master
Information System

Sales Channel Mgmt.
Information System

○ Applications

▢ Servers

Target Marketing
Information System

Order Acquisition
Information System

Other
Information Systems

Product Marketing
Information System

Figure 7–2
Linking information systems

If you draw all the potential linkages between information systems in a truly integrated enterprise, the picture isn't quite so pretty (see Figure 7–3).

This looks a lot like what we have in the legacy environment today. There is a better way. You didn't lose your metro pass did you? It's time to get back on the bus. Everyone aboard?

7.1.1 Formula for Direct Connections

There is a very simple mathematical formula that explains why the approach of direct connections between information systems is, in most cases, the wrong approach. You probably memorized this equation in high school and, after the final exam, relegated it to where you store other scholastic facts like all the state capitals in the United States.

$$\frac{n^2 - n}{2}$$

This is the equation that calculates the number of lines required to directly connect n points to each other. We can use this equation to calculate the number of direct connections that are needed between n things

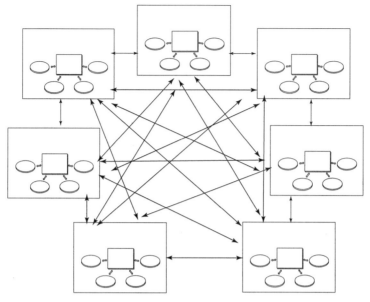

Figure 7–3
Potential linkages between information systems

of any kind. For example, if you wanted to connect the telephones in 100 homes directly with each other, you would need 4,950 direct connections (100 × 100 = 10,000; 10,000 − 100 = 9,900; 9,900 / 2 = 4,950). In this directly connected phone network, each phone would have 99 wires attached to it. Did the phone company do that? Of course not. As the network grew, it wired groups of homes to local stations and then eventually linked those stations to even larger stations, and so on, and so on, until it networked the entire world together with the fewest possible links.

If you wanted to network 100 computers together directly, you would again need 4,950 network connections, 99 to each computer. Would you do that? Of course not. You would add hubs and routers to the network.

If there were four remote farms in the wheat fields of Kansas and you needed to connect them with roadways, would you plow six direct roads (4 × 4 − 4) / 2 = 6 (see Figure 7–4)?

Of course not, you would build one road from each farm to an intersection somewhere in the middle (see Figure 7–5).

There is a different formula to calculate the number of connections for n points to a single point such as an intersection or hub. That formula is very simple. It is n.

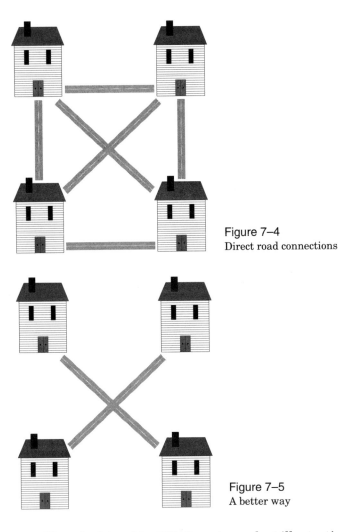

Figure 7–4
Direct road connections

Figure 7–5
A better way

If you had to add a fifth farm to our last illustration where the roads lead to an intersection, you would need only a single new road from the new farm to the intersection (see Figure 7–6). In the first case, where you plowed roads directly between each farm, you would have had to add four new roads, one to each of the original four farms from the new farm.

Our original equation was logarithmic. Logarithmic equations are dangerous. They look really innocent at first. But then they sneak up on you and, before you know it, they create huge numbers. This logarithmic equation is why it is not practical to connect information systems directly if we expect to achieve enterprise-wide information integration. In most

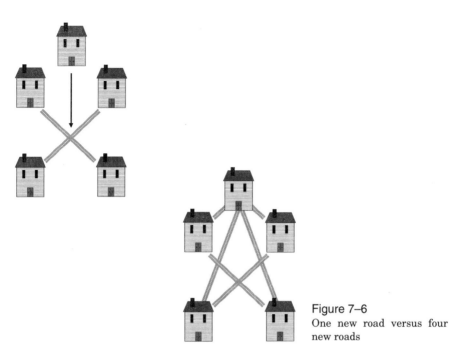

Figure 7–6
One new road versus four
new roads

companies, n will get to be a pretty big number, if it isn't already. We have several forces at work in the enterprise, each increasing the size of n and dramatically increasing the logarithmic results of our direct-connect equation.

7.1.1.1 n starts out pretty small When commercial computing was young, most companies had only one or two systems. Remember that the equation for connecting systems directly is sneaky:

$$\frac{n^2 - n}{2}$$

when $n = 2$, equates to

$$\frac{2^2 - 2}{2} = \frac{4 - 2}{2} = \frac{2}{2} = 1$$

(You probably don't need to use the equation to calculate the number of links between two systems.)

However, as the number of systems in the enterprise grows, the mathematics eventually causes a severe problem. Even in an architected environment, we already know that we will have multiple information systems in the enterprise, probably at least a couple for each original enterprise business function, plus several master reference data systems. If that's our only problem, n may stay small enough in uncomplicated companies to implement direct connections as a mechanism of integrating information systems, although you will still have quite a few links.

7.1.1.2 n gets bigger In large companies, it is likely that we will have multiple instances of each information system—in other words, multiple target marketing information systems. Even though we have succinctly defined the boundaries of an information system such as a target marketing information system, we didn't say you had to have only one of them for the whole company. Indeed, for business flexibility, you may decide that each of your primary product-line businesses needs or wants to use completely different application suites for its target marketing information system. (Remember that, although there may be many instances of the same information system, the automated functions and data within each still need to be within the boundaries of our definition of the target marketing information system.) Now you may need even more linkages. For example, the two target marketing information systems, one for each line of business within an enterprise, may still want to share data about prospects so they can cross-sell. Now the number of actual information systems, or n, is the total number of instances of each information system.

7.1.1.3 n gets even bigger Remember that each information system contains a tightly integrated set of applications and databases. In most legacy situations, different applications still require different databases, even within a single information system. For example, lead-generation and order entry applications may not necessarily want to be forced to use the same physical database, although we know they need to be tightly integrated because they are both within the boundaries of the order acquisition information system. Certainly different third-party software suppliers within the boundaries of a single information system usually require different data stores, although we know that, since they are in the same information system, we have to have a way to tightly integrate them. We'll most likely need to do that by linking those databases and applications together. Thus we have even more links to deal with. Now n is equal to the actual number of databases in each information system. Obviously you may not need to link all the databases to integrate the enterprise, but you probably need to link most of them. Look what happens as n gets bigger (see Figure 7–7).

n	Number of links between n
10	45
20	190
50	1,225
100	4,950
200	19,900
300	49,850
500	124,750

Figure 7–7
Results of n getting bigger

Certainly, not all databases in the legacy environment are connected today. But, in almost all cases, you can come up with a good business reason to link all of these information systems. For example, you may not think the personnel system needs to be linked to the sales channel management system. But if the sales rep getting commission on an order is an employee, these two systems will have to be linked so that the sales rep's commission can be added to his or her base salary. In many cases, the lack of some of these links causes most of the business problems in the enterprise that we would like to fix.

Some companies are small enough to manage a single instance of each information system in the enterprise, each with a single database (for example, one target marketing information system for the enterprise with a single physical database holding prospect data). With n remaining very low (perhaps ten or so), the number of links required for direct connection (forty-five) may be manageable. In some cases, companies can purchase an integrated suite of third-party modules that can automate more than one information system, such as finance, manufacturing, and order acquisition, on a single database. This reduces the number of links to a much smaller number.

To reduce the number of linkages you have to deal with, you may decide that the best approach is to create huge mainframe databases for one or all information systems. However, there are some very good reasons to avoid this approach. The obvious reasons include:

- You may not be able to handle required transaction volumes or throughput using this approach.
- The networking costs to access a single physical database from remote geographies may be prohibitive (for example, accessing a central database in the United States from Europe or Asia). In addition, network reliability from remote geographies may be an issue.

Among the not-so-obvious reasons (these are the ones that sneak up and bite you):

- This approach is not scalable. It may handle your current through-put, but if you outgrow it you may have to significantly change your entire technical architecture under emergency conditions.
- It makes it difficult to utilize multiple third-party applications within the boundaries of a single information system sharing a database since there are no known third-party applications that have completely compatible physical database structures.

These are the primary reasons why you should probably not design a technical architecture that requires single, enterprise-wide instances of each information system tightly integrated through single physical databases. It may simplify the architecture at first, but it has too many disadvantages.

7.2 So What's the Other Alternative to Integrate across Information Systems?

Our labyrinthine system linkages of today's architectures have crept up on us over the years. Remember, n started out as one. As soon as n started getting up around ten, we started having problems.

It is impossible to implement the number of direct links that would be necessary to truly integrate information across a large company (see Figure 7–8). That messy architecture that illustrates current informa-

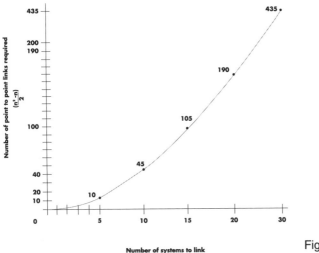

Figure 7–8

tion system linkages in your enterprise represents all of the futile attempts to do something, that for all practical purposes, is impossible. In fact, every direct link that we create between systems in large companies makes the task of replacing aging legacy systems just that much more difficult. Replacing a legacy system's functionality is usually not the problem; it is replacing all of the linkages the legacy system has to other legacy systems that makes it so difficult to complete a project like this.

There is a better way to connect information systems. It is not high tech. It's the same approach every other industry has used when the number of points they need to connect gets too large. This approach allows information systems to be integrated across the enterprise. But it reduces the number of spaghetti linkages between information systems and therefore streamlines the architecture. This approach also decouples each information system in such a way that applications within information systems or entire information systems can be replaced more quickly both during migration from the legacy architecture and in the future state. This decoupling allows a true plug-and-play architecture. Interested?

7.2.1 Information System Connectivity

In the legacy environment, information systems are usually connected together directly in one of two ways. The first is for one information system to send a copy of data to another information system, which then processes it and perhaps returns an updated copy of the data back to the sending information system. Most legacy information systems work this way using batch interfaces. The other method to directly connect information systems is to have one information system gain direct access to data in the other system so it can process it. This approach usually employs remote procedure call (RPC) or remote function call (RFC) technology.

For example, when our order acquisition system needs the prospect's name and address data created in the target marketing information system, we can have the order acquisition system directly access the prospect data in the target marketing information system. As another option, we can have the target marketing information system send a copy of the prospect data to the order acquisition system, which then utilizes its local copy for its order entry function and perhaps returns any changes to the prospect data back to the originating system (see Figure 7–9 for both examples).

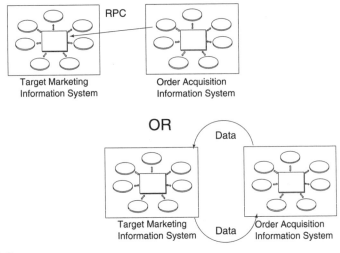

Figure 7–9
Ways to connect information systems

Both examples are solid approaches to connecting information systems. However, we want to modify these approaches slightly so that we can move away from direction connections and avoid the bramble bush that results.

In order to avoid direct connections where you are using RPCs or RFCs to directly access another information system's data, you will need some kind of standard format that all systems understand and probably some kind of enterprise-wide RPC routing function or gateway. This may be a very difficult architecture to pull off, given the heterogeneous environment of most legacy architectures today. It is also likely that, even in our future state, we may not be able to rely on enough consistency in the architecture to support this approach, especially if we are using multiple third-party vendors.

However, an RPC-oriented architecture has the least amount of data redundancy. We are not making copies of the data between information systems. In our example, the prospect database exists only in the target marketing information system, and the order acquisition system makes a remote call through an enterprise-wide gateway to gain access to it. We may not even have data redundancy in this type of architecture if we are going to have multiple-prospect databases within the boundaries of the target marketing information system. If, for example, we had four prospect databases for hardware and network performance reasons, we could partition the data into nonredundant data servers in this type of architecture. Perhaps we'd put prospects with last names beginning with A through E on one database and so on. Or perhaps we'd put European prospects on a database in Europe and Pacific Rim prospects on a database in Japan. If the calling information system, such as the U.S. order acquisition system, needed data about a European prospect, it would access the RPC routing mechanism which would know to go across the network to the server in Europe (see Figure 7–10). If it required data about a Pacific Rim prospect, it would go across the network to the server in the Pacific Rim.

There is probably a lot of appropriate skepticism about this approach. This may *never* be a practical architecture for some worldwide companies. Network costs, reliability, complexity of routing, and legacy systems are just some of the kinds of issues that get in the way of this architecture for some companies. Certainly, there are very few third-party applications that could fit into this kind of environment.

If RPCs won't work for your worldwide information system connectivity within your company, a replicated data architecture is probably a more practical approach. Replicated data gives the calling information system much more local control over the data it needs with the unfortunate tradeoff of replicated data management.

In our example, we would send a copy of the prospect data from the target marketing system to the order acquisition system. We could do this every few minutes, hourly, daily, weekly, monthly, or yearly depend-

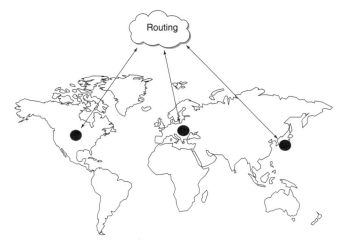

Figure 7–10
Routing data

ing on how important data synchronization is to us. Where we have only one instance of each information system, this works pretty easily.

But what if there were ten prospect databases held in multiple instances of the target marketing information systems, and what if they were distributed in countries all over the world? What if we have many order acquisition systems spread over the same geography that need copies of all or some of these databases? Now we're back to having to connect all of those systems together. In this environment, n is again too big to attempt direct connections through data replication.

Enter the idea of data hubs. It's the same approach as linking phones to a central station. This seems to be the most practical solution to the need to integrate a large number of information systems and databases across the enterprise. Data can sometimes be mastered directly in a single hub. However, usually data is mastered in the sourcing information system, replicated up to a data hub, and then replicated back to information systems that need access to that type of data. The data can also be replicated to local reference data stores that are not really part of any information system. These local data stores can then be available for all local information systems that need access to it—sort of a local data hub.

For example, the U.S. order acquisition system may need access to Pacific Rim and European prospects. With an enterprise hub in place, the Pacific Rim and European prospect data from their target marketing information systems are replicated to an enterprise prospect data hub and then replicated back to either the U.S. order acquisition system or a U.S. prospect server within the U.S. target marketing system or as a separate reference server (see Figure 7–11).

The arrows go both ways in this illustration, indicating that the Pacific Rim target marketing information system not only can replicate data *to* the enterprise hub but can receive replicated data back *from* the hub, for example if it needs access to European data.

The power of this approach is that data hubs solve several problems in our technical architecture. Hubs solve the problem of gaining access to data from another information system without worrying about multiple direct connections. They also solve the problem of gaining access to geographically distributed data within an information system—for example multiple target marketing systems that may need to share prospect data between them. So data hubs provide one-stop shopping to data both within and between information systems.

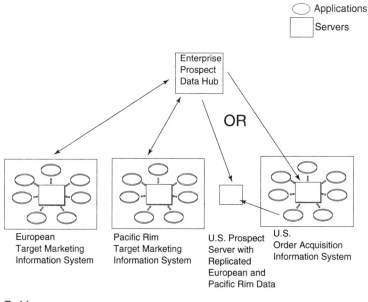

Figure 7-11
Using a data hub

Data hubs also make the architecture scalable. Now if we need to add additional target marketing systems or additional replicated copies of the prospect database because of company growth, the number of additional links to a hub is one per system, n new links for n new systems or databases.

Enterprise data hubs provide additional significant benefits.

- Data hubs decouple information systems from each other, allowing easier replacement of legacy systems or their replacements at some point.
- Data hubs allow easy integration of third-party software packages because of this decoupling.
- Data hubs provide one-stop shopping for integrated data for additional applications that haven't yet been thought of, such as decision support applications and data warehouses.

For those reasons, data hubs are solid, practical solutions to integrating the information architecture in your large enterprise. If you are in a smaller company, the single data servers within each information system become de facto data hubs without the data replication problems. Lucky you.

Remember that the concept of data hubs and the data replication approach they support introduces a problem of data redundancy that must be managed.

Data replication technology is on the bleeding edge right now, so you may have to do some of it yourself. However, it is making significant progress very quickly. Unfortunately, there are still some pretty severe limitations today. In most cases, all the replicated servers have to be the same database management system (DBMS), which makes it very difficult to implement this approach in a legacy environment.

Improving data replication technology is a top priority to all the key relational database vendors. "'A late 1994 survey of 50 information systems managers revealed that more than half were evaluating replication and that more than one-fourth had already committed to the technology,' according to Bobby Cameron, an analyst at Forrester Research, Inc., in Cambridge, Mass. 'But until Sybase and others offer sophisticated replication capabilities between their own databases and those of rivals, users are unlikely to adopt the technology across the board,' Cameron said."[1]

Many large companies have already built this type of data replication using batch technology. If you need real-time replication and synchronization between disparate database technologies, you may not want to attempt to build that yourself. Eventually the database vendors will provide it. Most likely, there will be a new set of standards in fairly short order to allow replication between different relational database management systems (RDBMS). At some point, one might envision that data would just sort of migrate around to local replicated servers based on patterns of usage and the DBMS will take care of it. (OK, I'm dreaming.)

However, if you don't want to wait around for any of this, you can go ahead and begin building your database hubs and replication mechanisms without too much trouble. It has already been done for some types of data in most large companies. If you build it yourself, make sure you leave complete flexibility for the data-sourcing information systems to utilize whatever database technology makes sense for the applications within their boundaries.

1. Kim Nash, "Replication Could Be Database Link," *Computerworld*, April 3, 1995: 69.

7.3 THIRD PARTIES FITTING INTO THE ARCHITECTURE

Almost all large companies built most of their mission critical applications from scratch a long time ago. These are what are typically called "legacy systems." However, it really doesn't make sense to build these large applications internally anymore unless you are in the software business and plan on selling them to recoup the incredible costs it takes to build these types of applications.

Most large companies haven't used third-party applications for mission critical applications because it is difficult to plug them into the maze of their existing architectures. Linking third-party applications to the rest of the legacy architecture usually requires all kinds of customization, which reduces the benefit of using a third party to start with. If we get rid of the tangled web of systems, it becomes much easier to plug a third-party solution into the enterprise architecture. This is one of the significant side benefits of data hubs.

There are several possible ways to plug third-party software solutions into our new architecture. Larger third parties can supply an entire information system with a central data server and a suite of integrated application modules. Medium-sized third parties can sometimes provide the central server and a subset of the applications within an information system. Smaller third parties can supply just one or two applications within an information system and usually require their own server that will need to be tightly integrated with other servers in the information system. In all cases, the data from the information system still needs to flow to the enterprise data hub for replication to other information systems that need access to it. Since the third-party applications have to know only about the data hubs, they don't need to know how to directly connect to the rest of the systems in the enterprise. It becomes much easier to utilize third parties in the new architecture. This is the plug-and-play capability that we discussed earlier. Let's discuss all three options in more detail (Figure 7–12).

Unfortunately, almost all third-party software suppliers have fallen into the same vertical development trap as most in-house development teams. Third-party data servers typically match the scope of their software, rarely the scope of an architected information system. Therefore, smaller third parties have servers that are only a subset of an information system; the largest third parties have servers that encompass multiple information systems. Neither is a desirable approach in an architected environment, but we do have some ways to work around these problems.

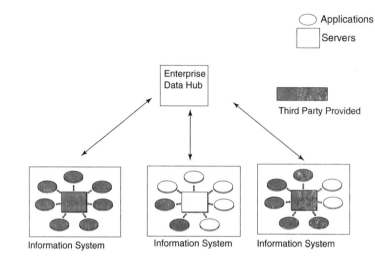

Figure 7–12
Options for plugging a third party into the architecture

7.3.1 Option One

The easiest way to plug a third party into the architecture is for it to provide all the functionality and data that match the boundaries of an information system. The data hubs provide the ability to replicate information between the third-party information systems and other internal or third-party information systems in the enterprise. Look to the largest commercial software houses to provide this type of solution set (Figure 7–13).

7.3.2 Option Two

Allow a third party to supply a single application within an information system. I haven't yet found very many third parties that have software that can work with someone else's database structure (either third party or in-house). Therefore, if they supply an application, most likely, they will supply a database server. For example, if you use two third-party suppliers for some applications within an information system and internal applications for the rest, you will probably end up with three databases for that information system. This is the hardest way to plug third parties into an architecture, but the hubs help out. In this case, the data hubs not only provide the ability to integrate with another information system, they also provide the ability to integrate information across applications within an information system (Figure 7–14).

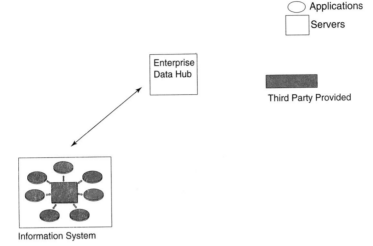

Figure 7–13
Option One: Possible third-party usage

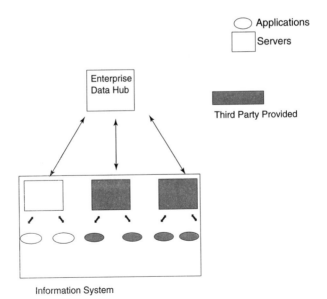

Figure 7–14
Option Two: Possible third-party usage

7.3.3 Option Three

If the third party doesn't meet all the application needs within an information system and *if* (and that's a big *if*) it has an open enough architecture for you to add data structures to its database and write additional clients to its server, it is pretty easy to plug it into the architecture. Third parties that have this kind of flexibility are probably going to be the most successful in the future (Figure 7–15).

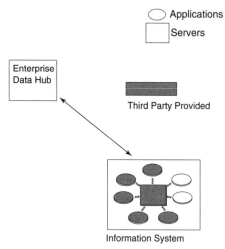

Figure 7–15
Option Three: Possible third-party usage

7.4 WE'RE DONE WITH THE BUSINESS VIEWS!

We have now completed all the business views of the architecture, including the technology architecture. In summary, we have defined the floor plan of the architecture by creating a streamlined set of information systems using classification theory. These information systems have the fewest possible links, but we have also defined a practical technical architecture to integrate information systems across the enterprise using data hubs.

7.5 REMAINING LEVELS OF THE ENTERPRISE INFORMATION ARCHITECTURE

Although we have completed the business views, there are a few things the business manager should know about remaining levels of the Zachman framework.

The business views of the architecture provide a conceptual set of information systems and linkages between those systems. As the lower levels of the architecture are fleshed out, systems will begin to be built, and more specific details about exactly where the boundaries of those systems are will come to light. The entities that we have been discussing are still fairly high-level groupings of data. In the lower levels of the architecture where actual database design occurs, those entities will decompose into many physical entities or tables in a database. For example, we would most likely show the entity *organizations* as a single entity in the data model for the business views of the architecture. In lower levels of the architecture, the data model will show more entities representing the data we need to know about an organization—perhaps the recursive relationship between organizational hierarchies and also the industries in which it operates.

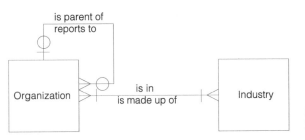

Figure 7–16
Lower-level data model

As these lower levels of the architecture are fleshed out, decisions are made about exactly which entities or data tables are within the boundaries of each information system so that databases can be designed.

7.5.1 Data Standards

We have already discussed that the boundaries of each information system are the first set of enterprise standards for the information architecture. In lower levels of the architecture, data standards will need to be set for actual fields of data within entities. Data element standards will need to be set only for fields of data that need to be shared between information systems. Since our data-sharing mechanism is the data hubs, these standards can be defined as part of the development of the data hubs.

As a reminder, standards increase flexibility by decoupling components from one another while still allowing interoperability. By creating succinct boundaries between information systems, we have decoupled them from one another to allow maximum flexibility. However, without enterprise data standards for information that needs to be utilized by multiple applications within an information system or an application that accesses information between information systems, the interoperability is lost.

Unfortunately, data standards are a lot of work. Data standards are set at the actual attribute or data field level, and as such setting them is very detailed and tedious work. Most companies have avoided them for this very reason. In today's environment, there is an incredible amount of redundant data. The same piece of data exists, of course in different formats, in many many databases. It has been said that, in Arabic, there are more than thirty different words for camel that have meanings such as pregnant camel and old male camel.[2] We have the same problem. In most companies, there are probably as many ways to define a single data element such as customer name or title as there are databases that hold the element. This may not seem to be a big problem, but it prevents us from integrating the architecture.

For example, the information system we called target marketing will most likely contain data elements that capture prospect profiles. For example, business-to-business marketing databases usually code prospects by job title categories. Let's assume that we have two physical database servers in our target marketing information system because a single one is impractical for our company. Each of these databases has a data field that is intended to code prospects by title. Let's look at two examples where we have data element incompatibility between these databases. In the first case, shown in Table 7–1, the field names in each

Table 7–1 Dual-element incompatibility

Database One: Field Name— Title Code		Database Two: Field Name— Manager Code	
Value	Meaning	Value	Meaning
01	President	5361a	President
02	Vice president	2933b	Vice president
03	Other manager	1333317	Other manager

2. Philip Davis and Rueben Hersch, *Descartes Dream, the World According to Mathematics*, 1986, p. 168.

database are different and the values are different, but the meanings are the same.

In this case, we really don't have much of a compatibility problem. If we wanted to send both data elements up to the hub for sharing across the enterprise, it wouldn't be difficult. Even though the field names are different and the values are different, the contents are compatible. It would certainly be easier if the developers used the same names and values, but it does not prevent us from integrating the information. The data hub could integrate these two data elements coming from two database sources by a simple one-to-one translation where 01 equals 5361a, and so on.

Now, let's take another situation, shown in Table 7–2. Let's say that these two databases have consistent field names and values but the meanings are different. If you send both of these data elements up to the hub, it can't make any sense of them. The data does not mean the same thing and is incompatible. No amount of translation fixes the problem.

What is important in setting data standards is the *meaning* of the field. Most enterprise data dictionary projects spend too much time on field names and values. Obviously, if it is possible to standardize on names and values, it helps. But it is compatibility in data field meaning that provides the true value to the enterprise.

Table 7–2 Dual-element incompatibility

First Database: Field Name— Title Code		Second Database: Field Name— Title Code	
Value	Meaning	Value	Meaning
01	President	01	President/vice president
02	Vice president	02	Other manager
03	Other manager/supervisor	03	Supervisor

7.5.2 Database Design Is Critical

Database design is extremely important and should not be left up to application programmers. It is *not* an art; it is a science. Database design is a completely different field of expertise from application programming. A good database designer should be educated in or knowledgeable about data structure theory, including the concept of normalization developed by Dr. E. F. Codd. Normalization basically removes data redundancy from the database design.

You can't fix all the database design problems in the legacy environment overnight. However, if you are setting data standards and building data hubs, take the time to do those right. There are several simple database design principles to remember.

7.5.2.1 One Field, One Fact   Let's illustrate why this is important to the business community. The following is a data field and its permitted values.

Field Name	Title Code
01	Vice president of marketing
02	Vice president of sales
03	Vice president of manufacturing
04	Vice president of personnel
05	Vice president of finance
06	Vice president of information systems

This field is intended to code prospects by the type of job that they hold. Now, what if you want to start creating new codes for the next level of management in each of those job functions? You need to add the following codes:

Field Name	Title Code
07	Division marketing manager
08	Division sales manager
09	Division manufacturing manager
10	Division personnel manager
11	Division finance manager
12	Division information systems manager

Do you see some creeping redundancy? The words marketing, sales, manufacturing, personnel, finance, and information systems appear twice. This is a classic example of poor data design. You see it everywhere in databases. There are two facts that we are currently collecting in this field of data. One has to do with the function the person is in, and the other has to do with his or her level of management. There should be two data fields—something like "job function" and "management level."

Field Name:	Job Function
01	Marketing
02	Sales
03	Manufacturing
04	Finance
05	Personnel
06	Information systems

Field Name:	Management Level
01	Vice president
02	Division manager

By ensuring that each field only has one fact, we *significantly* reduce redundancy and complication in the enterprise information architecture. This is why it is important to the business community. It's my opinion that all databases, unlike software, should go through a rigorous design approval process using extremely qualified experts.

7.5.2.2 *Never* Place Meaning in an Identifier   This is another phrase to remember when designing databases and setting data element standards. People place meaning in identifiers to make it easier for reporting or lookup purposes. However, placing meaning in an identifier almost always causes serious problems in the long term. Look at the following product identifier scheme. The first character of the product number is supposed to identify which product line the product belongs to, and the remaining characters are the product number.

Product No.	Meaning
1-223333	Product 223333 belongs to product line 1.
2-339393	Product 339393 belongs to product line 2.

Now, what happens when we have to merge with another company and need more than nine product lines? Of course by now there are hundreds of systems that utilize that first character to do lookups or reports. What happens when a product moves from one product line to another? We may actually have to change the product number and then spend the rest of our careers restating reports for that product line.

Unfortunately, data standards and database design happens further down the Zachman framework, and business people lose a lot of control over these activities. However, data standards and good database design are critical in order to actually implement an integrated information architecture. In fact, data standards are the integrating factor. Many reengineering efforts that need systems to integrate departments will fail without data standards. "If companies are to reap the full benefits of re-engineering, a key aspect of the process will be implementing corporate data standards, with a redefined and greatly reduced set of data elements."[3]

The importance of data standards and good database design is brought up in the business views because they are so important to the architecture. Some of the most important data elements are identifiers such as customer numbers or product numbers. The reason these are so important is that they allow the integration of a large amount of information. For example, a consistent customer number across target marketing databases that may be deployed by product line might allow the integration of a huge quantity of demographic profile information about prospects. When setting data standards, one data standard is better than none. As soon as you have agreed upon a data standard, publish it and begin using it in database structures. Don't create data standard projects that span months and years before delivering a single data standard. It may even be a good idea to set a few critical standards as part of the business views of the architecture. In many cases, it is obvious what the critical standard data elements are for each entity found in the business views.

7.6 ARE WE DONE YET?

Nope. We have completed the business views of the architecture, but we can't consider ourselves finished until we have figured out how to make the future-state architecture happen.

---

3. Max D. Hopper, "Time to Sharpen the Data Saw," *Computerworld*, February 20, 1995: 37.

CHAPTER 8

Making It Happen

We have completed the business views of the process, data, and technology architectures. But now we're at that awful place where we know what we have and we know what we want, but we don't know how to get from one place to the other. If we stay in this state for very long, we may get into trouble. Frustration or apathy sets in easily if there isn't a realistic way to get from one place to another more desirable place. We currently have a sprawling shantytown of information systems, and we have sketched our business views of a streamlined and integrated future-state architecture. To prevent frustration or apathy from gaining a foothold and stopping our forward momentum, we need a clear and realistic plan of action.

Fundamentally, there are three primary steps that need to taken immediately after creating the business views of the architecture.

- Step One: Take control of the current architecture. Step one is a *critical* step, but it is the one that is usually left out of most architecture projects. You need to take control of the current architecture or you will never get to your future architecture. Can you imagine trying to significantly remodel a home without any control over contractors who are constantly "fixing" parts of the home? It is unrealistic to expect that you will get to a future-state architecture if you allow uncontrolled modifications to the current legacy architecture. Very few companies can afford to ignore the legacy architecture and build an entirely new architecture in parallel. In fact, it is those modifications to the legacy architecture that will get you to the future state since most companies can't afford the risk of replacing all enterprise systems in a single project.

- Step Two: Set priorities. Almost all information systems organizations set some kind of priorities. However, in most cases, they are set in a very reactive manner. In an architected environment, priorities have to be set in a planned manner, again like remodeling a home. The foundation probably needs to be repaired before you make a significant investment in a new room that relies on that foundation. If your foundation is crumbling, but you have to have a new bathroom right away, that's OK. But it will be identified as a temporary structure according an appropriate amount of investment. If you make large investments in brand-new rooms before you fix the foundation, you're in for a lot of rework.

- Step Three: Chart the course. Establishing the course may seem to be a simple thing to do. After all, as managers, most of us have had to create tactical plans to meet a strategic objective before.

  Unfortunately, when moving to a new architecture, there is rarely a straight line in laying out the tactical plan to replace the legacy architecture with the future state. The reason for this is that, unlike the city of Denver, most of us don't have the ability to build a brand-new airport while we're still paying the mortgage on the one we already have. We also don't usually have the ability to stop the enterprise and move out into the streets while we remodel. So we're stuck. We have to remodel the architecture while we're still living in it.

  We have to come up with an approach to remodel our architecture that minimizes the risk to the enterprise. We do this by tacking toward our future architecture, much like a sailboat. Some of you may be disappointed that there isn't a more straightforward way to replace the legacy architecture with the new one. We could do this only if we could afford the risk and cost of replacing the whole thing at once. Since we usually can't afford that, we have to take the approach of tacking toward the future state.

  Tacking toward the future architecture does have some risk associated with it. The risk is that we will lose management commitment because it seems to take too long. However, having the business views of the architecture in place makes a big difference when it comes to retaining management support. Without a clear target, mutiny starts to seem like a pretty good option as the days drag on. With the business views of the architecture in place, the time it takes to tack toward the objective isn't such a big deal since management can see how to measure progress. Have we created enterprise data hubs? Have we reduced the number of direct linkages? Have we more tightly integrated legacy systems within information system boundaries? Have we decoupled systems that were spread across information system boundaries?

So charting a course involves defining a series of maneuvers, much like sailing maneuvers, that take us in the general direction of where we want to go, but give us the ability to minimize the risk and impact on the organization (Figure 8–1). Some of these tacks are temporary workarounds to fix urgent business problems or burning platforms. Others build foundational elements of the architecture that later tacks can take advantage of.

Unraveling the current architecture and getting the new floor plan in place will take time. In a very large company, it may take ten years or even more. Think of it as the major remodeling where you're knocking out walls and repairing the plumbing, electrical wiring, and foundation.

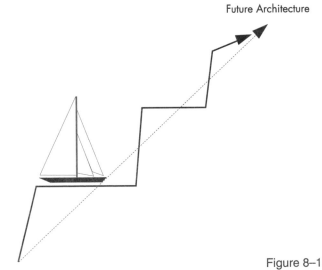

Future Architecture

Current Architecture

Figure 8–1
Tacking toward the future

At some point you will have a floor plan that works for your company. But don't forget—when we're done with our major remodeling and we're happy with our floor plan, we'll also have new paint and wallpaper. In other words, we'll likely have new technology in place. However, we will still expect to repaint and wallpaper periodically. These are the lower levels of Zachman's framework. We expect them to change over time.

The architecture is made up of the information systems boundaries and the enterprise data hubs and data standards that integrate those information systems. When you get your architectural components in place, you should be more proud of the floor plan of the remodeled house than you are of the wallpaper. The new technology is not the important part of the architecture. If you think that the new technology is your architecture, you are automatically assuming that your architecture will not stand the test of time. "Gartner Group has the 3/24 rule. It says that virtually no technology solution will be competitive after three years. But at the same time, businesses want an economic return for technology investments in 24 months."[1] This is a pretty impossible ratio to maintain. Economic return will occur because your architecture is in place to enable new technologies to be deployed on a regular basis with minimal investment because the infrastructure is already in place. After the floor plan is in place, you will only have to buy a new car occasionally, not build a new interstate highway to go along with it.

Let's go into a little more detail on how to perform the three critical migration steps.

8.1 STEP ONE: TAKE CONTROL OF THE CURRENT ARCHITECTURE

Remember our earlier discussion about assets? Information system investments are in many cases *the* most expensive assets in the company, costing in some cases millions of dollars in hardware, software, and maintenance costs. However, they are rarely controlled as assets. No wonder they don't get much business attention. Taking control means treating information systems as assets. If you want to take control, it's time to enlist the controller of your company. Figures, doesn't it?

8.1.1 Information Systems as Assets

If your controller is like most controllers, you probably have a fairly strict asset management process where assets are logged and tracked

1. Allan Alter, "Myth of Long-Term Planning," *Computerworld*, October 17, 1994: 97.

through their life cycle, most likely in some kind of automated fashion. In most companies, assets as small as a thousand dollars are tracked. It's almost incredible that, although there probably isn't one significant database or application in our enterprise that cost less than one hundred thousand dollars, we don't even know where they all are!

8.1.2 Ally Ally In Come Free!

It's time to call for an enterprise-wide inventory of information systems assets. I can already hear the excuses why this won't work. This request, no, this directive, should come from executive business management to your controller to your information systems community. The information systems community should perform the inventory on behalf of the controller because they usually have some idea of where these things are. Ignore the excuses. Information systems are assets worthy of a regular inventory. Just accept the fact that no one volunteers for an inventory any more than one volunteers to go to the dentist. It's a required asset management process, no more, no less.

It's important to come up with an information system asset management process that will stand the test of time so that you don't have to reinventory the same systems next month because you did it wrong the first time. This is why your company controller is so helpful. Utilize existing, tested asset management processes where possible. This also positions information systems as the same as the rest of the expensive assets in your company that need to be managed.

Like all asset management processes, you probably want to consider just how large the asset has to be before you'll inventory it. Hopefully, you won't decide to inventory every departmental PC database or Lotus spreadsheet, for example. Although you don't want to change your asset management process regularly, it is a good idea to limit what you will inventory the first time and expand what is considered to be an information system asset over time. If you're in a large company, maybe you should start out by limiting the inventory to systems that run on certain larger hardware platforms or cost a certain amount of money to maintain. It's important not to bog down the asset management process by attempting to control everything in the first year.

In the interest of separating data, process, and technology, start out right by inventorying data assets (databases) separate from software (process) assets and separate from hardware assets (technology). This is a little difficult to do because we don't think that way today. For example, because of the past vertical orientation to system design (one database, one application), most current databases don't even have a name, since they are usually assumed to be the same thing as the application. Either give each database a new name or tack some kind of prefix or suffix to the name to distinguish them as separate assets. If you need to reduce the amount of effort in your first inventory, focus on the databases first!

If you have time to do it at all, just make sure you separate the components. For example, if you have one of those typical vertical systems called SAFIRE that includes an application and a database and you have three copies of it in your company running on different computers, call the application SAFIRE, the database SAFIRE-DB, and the three computers SAFIRE-COMP1, 2, and 3. Better yet, rename the database something completely different like EMERALD and the computers CURLY, MO, and LARRY. This sounds so trivial, but it is important! We are beginning the important process of decoupling data from process from technology in our enterprise information architecture. The SAFIRE-DB and computers will not necessarily be utilized only by the SAFIRE application in the future state. By labeling an application, its database, and its computers with the same name, we are subtly encouraging vertical approaches to system design.

Significant system interfaces should also be inventoried. If SAFIRE includes a large database, an on-line transaction processing (OLTP) application, and ten more significant batch applications that move its data around to other systems, and it involves three computers, you need fifteen lines in your asset inventory to cover the SAFIRE system. Of course, if other applications are running on SAFIRE's computers or using those same batch links, you would only inventory them once.

This approach actually makes it easier to do an information system asset inventory. A few companies have tried to inventory their information system assets without separating data from application from hardware. Typically there is a lot of overlap in the inventory due to confusion over which applications, interfaces, databases, and computers should be included as a single system.

Asset management processes usually track the valuation of the asset. This is sometimes difficult to do for information system assets since maintenance is such a high component of the cost, especially of internally designed software. The primary goal of our inventory is just to figure out what we have and where it is, not to track costs. This is where you may have to keep your controller at bay. If you do wish to begin to understand your information system costs, you may have to work out an appropriate way to track asset value. However, since it is critical to separate data assets from software assets from technology assets to gain control of the architecture, you may not be able to log a dollar amount per asset because of the way most companies vertically account for information system costs. For example, rarely are database costs separated from the cost of the application.

As an example, you probably can estimate that the SAFIRE system costs approximately one million dollars to run and maintain each year. But it would most likely be difficult to allocate that million dollars to each of SAFIRE's fifteen components. Therefore, if you do want to track costs, the valuation estimate will probably need to be tracked for a group of assets. Once you truly manage data separate from application separate from technology, eventually you can begin to track costs this way. Don't require it for now because at best people will probably just dream up arbitrary allocations that will lower the overall importance of the asset inventory.

The information systems inventory should not take very long if it is planned correctly and you are clear as to what information you want to collect about each component. However, even if it does take you awhile, it can be done in parallel with other activities that help you take control over the current architecture. Don't wait until after you have completed the inventory to initiate other controlling steps. In fact, you can start the inventory even before you begin building the business views of the architecture. The faster you gain control over your current architecture, the faster you will move toward your future architecture.

8.1.3 Enterprise Data Standards

As we've discussed before, the concept of standards is the key to interconnectivity in most industries, including commercial information processing. The boundaries of our information systems have already become our first set of enterprise information architecture standards. Even a carefully scoped set of information systems will remain as islands of information if the data that needs to flow between them is incompatible. This is why enterprise data standards are so important.

Remember that standards are not always perfect in the beginning and that not everything has to be standard. Data standards bodies can easily be lulled into becoming theoretical think tanks and can spend years locked up in rooms arguing about minutiae. Remember that important standards have been driven by urgent situations like war, danger, and significant business opportunities. Let urgent business situations drive the priorities for your standards bodies.

To get started on data standards, assign someone or a group of people to be responsible for them. Then align that person or group with an important system development effort, one that is addressing a significant business problem or a large piece of the architecture. The best way to start is to gain sponsorship for a data hub and start your data standards effort as part of this project. This way the standards effort can be positioned as assisting a system development effort as opposed to hindering it. The standards and data modeling work should just be considered part of the database design effort for the system. Many companies are finding that this is a much more pragmatic approach to an enterprise data standards effort. "We didn't model all of the data before we did anything—just what we needed at the time," states Jack Spurgeon, Eastman Chemical Company's vice president of computing systems.[2]

After data standards have been identified as part of a completed database design, the standards effort can move on to the next significant system development effort. Once the enterprise data standards cover a broad number of information systems and become an accepted part of every development effort, you can separate the standards effort from any particular development effort.

Remember that not all fields in every system should be considered enterprise standards. Enterprise data standards should be identified only where the value of interoperability with other information systems exceeds the value of uniqueness. If you start by building data hubs, you get the benefit of identifying what data needs to be shared, and therefore standardized as part of the analysis phase of the data hub project.

8.1.4 Reducing the Number of Databases

Taking control means having an asset inventory of all your databases, software, and hardware and a set of enterprise data standards that will eventually be required in every development effort. However, you may still have a problem gaining control of your current architecture. This is because there are still too many uncoordinated development efforts going on in most enterprises. We'll eventually remedy this situation because our future information systems will demand much more integration between development teams operating within their bound-

2. Avery Jenkins, "Data Modeling: One Bit at a Time," *Computerworld Client/Server Journal*, February 1995: 45.

aries. However, we may need to take aggressive, short-term action to begin to rein in the current architecture.

One of the main problems with current architectures is that there are too many databases. This situation has been caused by the vertical alignment of software to database. This usually causes a tremendous amount of data redundancy which in turn causes data quality problems. Since no one can trust anyone else's data, everyone creates even more databases and applications as workarounds. The best way to gain control over the current architecture is to begin to tightly rein in database development, not application development.

If you are in a large company, you probably have multiple applications within the boundaries of an information system defined in the business views of the future-state architecture (Figure 8–2).

As you sit here reading this book, there is at least one project starting up somewhere in your organization that will significantly enhance or replace a current application. Of course, the plans are to replace it one for one—a new application *and* a new proprietary database (Figure 8–3).

Stop! Don't miss this opportunity to take your first tack toward your future architecture. You already have a good idea of the boundaries of your information systems developed in the business views of the architecture. If someone needs to significantly enhance or replace a current application with a proprietary database, *strongly* encourage or *require* them to team up with an organization that has a database or databases within the same information system boundary. Replace or enhance the

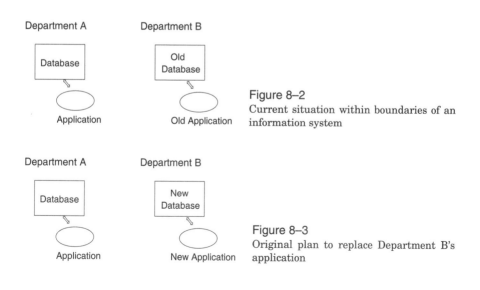

Department A   Department B

Database   Old Database

Application   Old Application

Figure 8–2
Current situation within boundaries of an information system

Department A   Department B

Database   New Database

Application   New Application

Figure 8–3
Original plan to replace Department B's application

department's database(s) to meet both organizations' needs while still allowing each organization to develop its own application if it makes sense to do so (Figure 8–4).

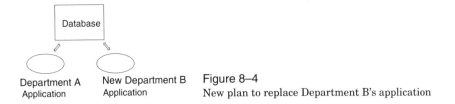

Department A   New Department B   **Figure 8–4**
Application   Application   New plan to replace Department B's application

After fifty years of uncontrolled commercial information system development, most new development efforts are replacing functionality or data that can already be found in some form elsewhere in the enterprise. Of course, that form is not the form that a new development team wants it in, which is why they want to do their own thing. Don't stop them from developing an application; just encourage them to team up with another department with similar needs within the boundary of an information system. Reducing the number of databases until we have a good idea of how we will get to the new architecture is an aggressive but pragmatic way to rein in the current architecture without requiring users to give up the need for improved automation.

Figure 8–4 may look a little familiar. You may remember our earlier illustrations of the intended use of database technology, that of separating code from data. This is the exact same approach you will take to unraveling the current legacy spaghetti architecture. Rather than waiting until you have all your priorities and road map in place, you can get started unraveling right away by eliminating databases within information systems boundaries and forcing multiple applications to use the same database. There used to be a heavily used abbreviation describing how to simplify a process—ESA for eliminate, simplify, automate. By eliminating databases (not necessarily applications), you take the first step toward the new streamlined architecture.

8.2 STEP TWO: SET PRIORITIES

8.2.1 Architecture Dependencies

When builders set priorities, they look at what needs to be done and figure out, holistically, what should be done first in order to minimize rework. They have to look at the whole project, in our case the entire architecture, before they can make good decisions about where to start. In an architected environment, information systems that create data need to be rebuilt before rebuilding the information systems that will utilize that data. These systems are the "foundation" of our new architecture. If you were using a CASE tool and were further down the Zachman framework and could load the enterprise CRUD matrix, it could actually calculate information system dependencies, determining which information system to rebuild first.

It isn't necessary to use a CASE tool to determine information system priorities. To find your lowest-priority systems, decide which information systems can't work without data created in other information systems. Priority in this sense doesn't mean that they aren't important; it just means that, to really fix them, you have to fix the upstream systems first. After finding your lowest-priority systems, the systems that are remaining are the foundation of the architecture. These will typically be systems that create foundation data like prospect data or data about your market offerings (products). All this data is critical before you can create an order; therefore order acquisition systems are typically the most dependent on upstream systems. If you try to fix the downstream systems first, you will most likely have severe scope-creep problems because of the upstream problems that also need to be addressed before you can make the impact that you want. Unfortunately, many "burning platforms" that become reengineering initiatives are within the boundaries of downstream information systems, and this is probably the main reason for the high failure rate of technology-enabled reengineering initiatives. If you can simultaneously fix the upstream problems and downstream problems, then you may still be OK.

Typically, the foundation systems end up being systems that are called reference systems such as systems that manage the "product file" or "customer file." In almost all commercial enterprises that have developed the business views of an architecture, the highest priorities are the customer and product reference systems since so many downstream business problems are caused by problems in these systems. From an article about Apple Computer's information architecture team, "After conducting a series of focus groups with key user representatives, the team identified five problems deemed important enough to discuss with the executive management team. Then, the executives determined that the issues related to the product domain should be addressed first, followed by work on the customer domain."[3]

3. Ron Carnahan, "How Apple Computer's Information Architecture Group Uses Reusable Data Models to Standardize Its Customer and Product Data," *DBMS*, August 1993: 44.

As we've seen in developing our architecture, there are even higher-level reference systems that need to exist such as those "master information systems" that were not wholly owned within any particular information system. If you recall, we discovered one when we were developing the business views of the sales and marketing functions and called it the organization master information system.

If we were to order the rest of the information systems within the sales and marketing functions, we would again look at dependencies. You don't need a CASE tool to figure this out. Think of the overall business itself and how it got started. It is pretty obvious that we probably created markets, market offerings, and probably sales channels before we created customer orders. Since we haven't yet completed the full suite of information systems for all enterprise business functions, we may find that some of the information systems in sales and marketing rely on data created even earlier in other functions.

Most of our serious business problems usually crop up in the downstream information systems. Unfortunately, since the business problem is pretty important, we all rush off to fix the downstream system, somewhat like the children in a soccer game, where all the players can be found three feet from the ball, even when it's out of bounds. If your downstream problems are burning platforms, your plan will have to deal with fixing the downstream business problems while still allowing you to fix the root causes of the problem, probably found upstream. However, remember that those downstream, quick-fix systems will likely have to be significantly changed or even replaced at some point.

8.3 STEP THREE: CHART THE COURSE

The next step is to chart the course or identify a series of tacks that we'll take to migrate to the new architecture.

8.3.1 Isolating and Decoupling Legacy Systems through Data Hubs

Once we know what our priorities are, the first thing we need to do is use those priorities to start unraveling the information system morass. Let's go back to the analogies we used to demonstrate the direct link problem that we currently have in our architecture.

Remember, we found that if we wanted to connect five things directly, we would need

$$\frac{n^2 - n}{2}$$

or ten connections. If we had a directly connected telephone network, it would look like that in Figure 8–5.

How would we unravel this mess if we want to decouple these direct connections? It's actually quite easy. The first thing we do is wait until we have a funded opportunity to rewire just one link between two homes. In our example, we'll assume that house 1 and house 3 need new wiring. We use this opportunity to invest a little extra, create a hub and link just those two homes to it. All the homes still have four wires each, but now we're set up to make a logarithmic reduction in links.

The first time you create a hub, you actually make the job a little harder, which makes it difficult to gain support for this approach. Notice that there are now eleven links in our architecture, not ten.

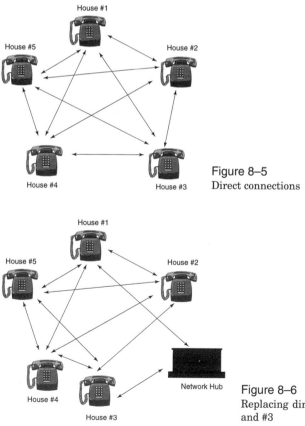

House #1
House #5
House #2
House #4
House #3

Figure 8–5
Direct connections

House #1
House #5
House #2
House #4
House #3
Network Hub

Figure 8–6
Replacing direct link between house #1 and #3

However, the next time you have an opportunity to rewire the direct connection between two more homes—for example houses 2 and 5—you connect them to the existing hub, and they now automatically get links to the two additional homes already linked to the hub—houses 1 and 3. Now you can delete all those direct connections between those four houses because they are now redundant. Look how much cleaner the picture already looks (see Figure 8–7).

In *one* more step, we will have completely unraveled our tangled architecture. We just need to link house 4 to the hub which will give it access to the rest of the four homes. Now we can delete the remaining four redundant links (see Figure 8–8).

The incredible benefit of this approach is it reverses the exponential nature of the connection equation

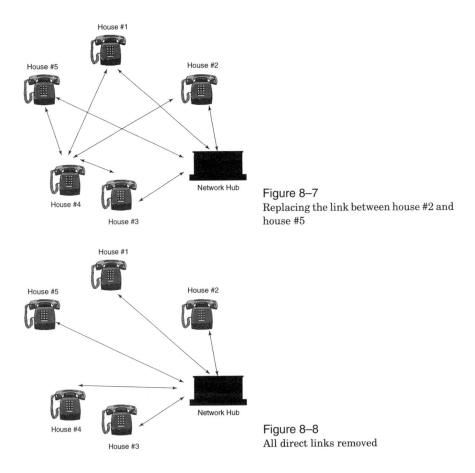

Figure 8–7
Replacing the link between house #2 and house #5

Figure 8–8
All direct links removed

$$\frac{n^2 - n}{2}$$

As fast as you increase the number of linkages when using the direct linkage approach, you can decrease the number of direct linkages by using hubs.

We'll use the same approach for our course to the future state. If we have a need to replace or enhance a link between applications, we will take the opportunity to build the beginnings of an enterprise data hub (or hubs if the data needs are across information systems) that spans at least the data the two applications need to share. Since we have to rewrite the links anyway, we just write the links to the hub instead of to each other. When each opportunity arises to rewrite links between systems, we either create or enhance a data hub to support the need. Then we write the links to the hub. At some point, we will not have to create or enhance a hub; we will need only to write the link.

By taking the hub approach and unraveling the direct links between systems, we will be able to easily isolate and replace critical legacy systems. The problem with replacing mission critical legacy systems in today's unarchitected environment is that they typically have many, many direct links to other legacy systems (Figure 8–9). These links have built up over twenty or thirty years, and it is almost *impossible* to replace

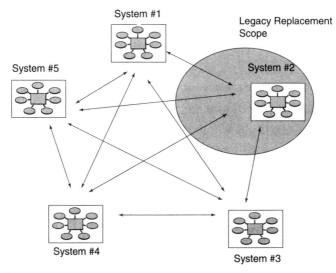

Figure 8–9
Replacing legacy systems in a directly connected architecture is difficult

all that functionality in one project. That is why those replacement projects have incredible scope problems and a huge failure rate.

The most pragmatic way to isolate and replace critical legacy systems that have many direct links is to take away some of those direct links first using the data hub approach (Figure 8–10). Eliminate links and then replace the legacy system. Once you have reduced the number of direct links to the legacy system, you reduce the scope of the replacement project.

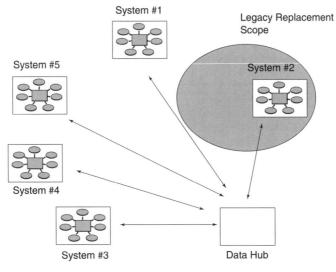

Figure 8–10
Eliminate, simplify, and replace

8.3.2 Warehouses and Decision Support Systems as Interim Integrators

Up to this point, we have focused only on the operational data processing needs of an enterprise. During the late 1980s, the concept of decision support systems emerged to meet the business analysis needs of the enterprise. Up to that point, the information needs of management had really been ignored in favor of meeting the needs of transaction processing.

A decision support architecture is made up of a set of data warehouses and software tools that analyze data held in the warehouses. Just as OLTP characterizes the type of software used against operational databases, on-line analytical processing (OLAP) characterizes the software used in the decision support environment against data warehouses. What is a data warehouse? "A data warehouse is a database that provides users with data, extracted from production and on-line transaction processing systems, that supports business analysis activities."[4] The source of data for a data warehouse is the operational architecture. In other words, the operational architecture feeds the data warehouse. In general, data from the operational architecture is integrated in the warehouse, providing information out of data.

It is not possible to go into enough detail to totally describe the data warehouse environment at this point. Suffice it to say that it is significantly different than the operational environment that we have been discussing so far. However, it is important to understand that the common rule in the industry today is that you should not mix the operational and decision support environments. You may have systems in your company where you have attempted to do this by performing data analysis directly against a transaction processing database. The data in operational types of databases is structured for transaction processing, not search and retrieval. The leading industry expert on warehouses, Bill Inmon, gives several important reasons to keep these two architectures separate: "The split of operational and informational databases occurs for many reasons:

- The data serving operational needs are physically different data from those serving informational or analytic needs.
- The supporting technology for operational processing is fundamentally different from the technology used to support informational or analytical needs.
- The user community of operational data is different from the one served by informational or analytical data.
- The processing characteristics for the operational environment and the informational environment are fundamentally different.

Because of these reasons, the modern way to build an architecture is to separate operational and informational or analytical processing and data."[5]

4. Avery Jenkins, "Warehouse Woes," Computerworld, February 6, 1995: 102.
5. *Building the Data Warehouse*, 1992, p. ix.

8.3.2.1 Benefit of Warehouses   Although you should not mix the operational and analytical environments, there are a lot of very important benefits of a data warehouse. They include the following:

1. The first benefit of a warehouse is that it is targeted to meet the needs of management. It is an easy way to engage business management's interest in information systems. The information that is in a warehouse allows business managers to make better decisions—for example, better target marketing decisions, better asset management decisions—and gain better customer understanding.

2. A warehouse project raises the visibility of significant problems in the operational architecture. Right after management gets excited about the possibilities of better decision support through integrated data in the warehouse, they'll discover that there are significant problems in the quality and compatibility of the sourcing data. This helps gain support for fixing these problems.

3. A warehouse can buffer you from some of the data quality and compatibility problems in the legacy operational architecture. In order to build a warehouse, you may not have to fix all the problems in the sourcing operational system right away. Some incompatible or dirty data can be transformed, cleaned, and synchronized after being pulled from the operational environment and before loading it into the warehouse. This allows you to get past some of the legacy data quality problems in the short term.

4. Since you probably don't already have a legacy data warehouse, you get to start with a clean slate and do things right! When building a warehouse, for once you get to create a data model without considering the legacy environment. In many cases, this is a good place to create the enterprise data model and identify data standards.

8.4 MANAGING THE ARCHITECTURE

We know we don't want to control all information system development resources centrally. That paradigm broke down a long time ago as technology became pervasive in the enterprise. However, managing an enterprise information architecture will require some sort of central control. Earlier, we talked about Peter Drucker's concept of federation which included both strong parts and a strong center. This is a good model for managing the architecture. A federation balances power and authority between central and decentralized bodies of government. The United States is a federation of states with the balance of power managed through a constitution. A federated approach to managing the architecture would most likely place the definition and management of the business views of the architecture centrally. The definition and management of the lower levels of the architecture where systems are actually created are better decentralized, although the business views of the architecture places constraints on them. Potentially, data hubs should be managed centrally even down through their physical implementation in lower levels of the architecture. The federated approach to managing the architecture allows central authority with decentralized deployment, a true balance of power in the enterprise.

8.5 THERE YOU HAVE IT!

Today's commercial information system architectures, if you can call them that, not only don't integrate the enterprise, they are *dis*integrating the enterprise. Designing and implementing a streamlined, integrated enterprise information architecture is not that difficult. First, define information systems boundaries based on classification theory so that each information system has the fewest possible tentacles into other information systems. Then design a technology architecture that links these information systems using hubs to minimize the number of links even further.

To migrate as quickly as possible to the future-state architecture, treat information systems as assets and take immediate control of the current architecture. Especially control new database design and deployment during the migration because it is the foundation of the architecture. Set migration priorities based on information system dependencies. Set data standards and build data hubs to begin decoupling legacy information systems from each other so they can be more easily replaced. Build warehouses to provide decision support information to meet the immediate needs of management.

There are very few good ideas that haven't already been thought of. Mathematics, classification theory, architectural design, standards, ... these are the mothers of invention. These ancient concepts are still incredibly useful in the information age.

We're at the fifth station. Everyone out. The bus stops here.

Bibliography

Bell, Eric Temple, *Mathematics, Queen & Servant of Science*, New York: McGraw-Hill Book Company, Inc., 1951.

Bender, Tex, *Don't Squat with Yer Spurs On! A Cowbow's Guide to Life*, Layton, UT: Gibbs Smith, 1992.

Betts, Mitch, "Census 2000 Gears up with Systems Overhaul," *Computerworld*, October 3, 1994.

Bidgoli, Hossein, *Decision Support Systems, Principles and Practice*, St. Paul, Minn.: West Publishing Company, 1989.

Bloom, Benjamin S., *Taxonomy of Educational Objectives*, New York: David McKay Company, Inc., 1956.

Bracket, Michael H., *Practical Data Design*, Englewood Cliffs, N.J.: Prentice-Hall, Inc., 1990.

Brady, Robert A., *Organization, Automation, and Society: The Scientific Revolution in Industry*, Berkeley, Calif.: University of California Press, 1961.

Bray, Olin H., *Distributed Database Management Systems*, Lexington, Mass.: D. C. Heath and Company, 1982.

Bruce, Thomas A., *Designing Quality Databases with IDEF1X Information Models*, New York: Dorset House Publishing, Inc., 1992.

Brumbaugh, Robert S., *Plato for the Modern Age*, New York: Crowell-Collier Press, 1962.

Byrne, John A., "The Horizontal Corporation, It's about Managing Across, Not Up and Down," *Newsweek*, December 20, 1993.

Carroll, Lewis, *Lewis Carroll's Symbolic Logic*, edited by William Warren Bartley III, New York: Clarkson N. Potter, Inc., 1977.

Champdor, Albert, *Babylon*, London: Elek Books Ltd., 1958.

Chang, Chin-Liang, and Richard Char-Tung Lee, *Symbolic Logic and Mechanical Theorem Proving*, Boston, Mass.: Academic Press, Inc., 1973.

Coad, Peter, and Edward Yourdon, *Object-Oriented Analysis*, Englewood Cliffs, N.J.: Prentice-Hall, Inc., 1990.

Davis, Philip J., and Reuben Hersch, *Descartes' Dream, the World According to Mathematics*, San Diego, Calif.: Harcourt Brace Jovanovich, Inc., 1986.

Donovan, John J., *Crisis in Technology*, Cambridge, Mass.: Cambridge Technology Group, 1990.

Draffan, I. W., and F. Pool, *Distributed Data Bases*, Cambridge: Cambridge University Press, 1980.

Dreyfus, Hubert L., *What Computers Still Can't Do: A Critique of Artificial Reason*, Cambridge, Mass.: MIT Press, 1992.

Drucker, Peter F., *The Practice of Management*, New York: Harper, 1954.

Evans, Christopher, *The Micro Millennium*, New York: Viking Press, 1980.

Finkelstein, Clive, *Strategic Systems Development*, Singapore: Addison-Wesley Publishing Company, 1992.

Flesch, Rudolph, *The Art of Clear Thinking*, New York: Harper, 1951.

Gessford, John E., *How to Build Business-Wide Databases*, New York: John Wiley & Sons, 1991.

Goldberg, Robert, and Harold Lorin, *The Economics of Information Processing*, Vol. 1, *Management Perspectives*, New York: John Wiley & Sons, 1982.

Gorman, Michael M., *Enterprise Database in a Client/Server Environment*, New York: John Wiley & Sons, 1994.

Hamilton, Edith, *The Greek Way*, New York: W. W. Norton & Company, 1930.

Hammer, Michael, and James Champy, *Reengineering the Corporation: A Manifesto for Business Revolution*, New York: HarperBusiness, 1993.

Hudnut, Joseph, *Architecture and the Spirit of Man*, Cambridge: Harvard University Press, 1949.

Inmon, W. H., *Building the Data Warehouse*, Boston, Mass.: Technical Publishing Group, 1992.

Inmon, W. H., *Data Architecture, the Information Paradigm*, 2d ed., Boston, Mass.: Technical Publishing Group, 1992.

Inmon, W. H., *Developing Client/Server Applications in an Architected Environment*, Boston, Mass.: Technical Publishing Group, 1991.

Jeffrey, C., *An Introduction to Plant Taxonomy*, Cambridge: Cambridge University Press, 1982.

Jenkins, Avery, "Data Modeling: One Bit at a Time," *Computerworld Client/Server Journal*, February, 1995.

Jenkins, Avery, "Warehouse Woes," *Computerworld*, February 6, 1995.

Kast, Fremont E., and James E. Rosenzweig, *Organization and Management, a Systems Approach*, New York: McGraw-Hill, Inc., 1970.

Martin, James, *Information Engineering*, Bk. I, *Introduction*, Englewood Cliffs, N.J.: Prentice-Hall, Inc., 1989.

Martin, James, *Information Engineering*, Bk. II, *Planning & Analysis*, Englewood Cliffs, N.J.: Prentice-Hall, Inc., 1990.

Mayer, Raymond R., *Production and Operations Management*, New York: McGraw-Hill, Inc., 1982.

Mitchell, Russell, "Fantastic Journeys in Virtual Labs," *Business Week*, September 19, 1994.

Monks, Joseph G., *Operations Management: Theory and Problems*, New York: McGraw-Hill, Inc., 1977.

Moravec, Hans P., *Mind Children, the Future of Robot and Human Intelligence*, Cambridge, Mass.: Harvard University Press, 1988.

Morrison, Phillip and Emily, *Charles Babbage and His Calculating Engines*, New York: Dover Publications, Inc., 1961.

Morton, Michael Scott, *The Corporation of the 1990s, Information Technology and Organizational Transformation*, New York: Oxford University Press, 1991.

Nesmith, Achsah, "A Long, Arduous March toward Standardization," *Smithsonian Magazine*, March 1985.

Parsaye, Kamran, Mark Chignell, Setrag Khoshafian, and Harry Wong, *Intelligent Databases, Object-Oriented, Deductive, Hypermedia Technologies*, New York: John Wiley & Sons, 1989.

Penzias, Arno, *Ideas and Information, Managing in a High-Tech World*, New York: W. W. Norton & Co. Inc., 1989.

Roszak, Theodore, *The Cult of Information*, New York: Pantheon Books, 1986.

Runge, Larry, "Getting a Truly Customer-driven System Calls for Nothing Short of Starting from Scratch," *Computerworld*, October 24, 1994.

Scheer, A. W., *Enterprise-Wide Data Modelling, Information Systems in Industry*, Heidelberg: Springer-Verlag Berlin, 1989.

Shaffner, George, "Redefining Open Systems," *Computerworld*, July 4, 1994.

Spewak, Steven, *Enterprise Architecture Planning*, Boston: QED Publishing Group, 1993.

Stace, Clive A., *Plant Taxonomy and Biosystematics*, 2d ed. E. Arnold, 1989.

Stuessy, Tod F., *Plant Taxonomy, the Systematic Evaluation of Comparative Data*, New York: Columbia University Press, 1990.

Tom, Paul L., *Computer Information Systems, a Managerial Approach*, Glenview, Ill.: Scott, Foresman & Co., 1989.

U.S. Congress, Office of Technology Assessment, *Global Standards: Building Blocks for the Future*, Washington, D.C.: U.S. Congress, Office of Technology Assessment, 1992.

U.S. Department of Commerce, National Bureau of Standards, *Guide to Distributed Database Management*.

Van Doren, Charles, *A History of Knowledge*, New York: Ballantine Books, 1991.

Veryard, Richard, *Information Modelling, Practical Guidance*, London: Prentice-Hall, Inc., 1992.

Von Oech, Roger, *A Whack on the Side of the Head; How to Unlock Your Mind for Innovation*, New York: Warner Books, Inc., 1983.

Watterson, Joseph, *Architecture, a Short History*, New York: W. W. Norton & Company, 1968.

Zachman, John A., "A Framework for Information Systems Architecture," *IBM Systems Journal* 26, no. 3, 1987.

Index